W9-AYR-587

The American Civil War

DATE DUE

THE AMERICAN CIVIL WAR
A Multicultural Encyclopedia

PRODUCED BY THE PHILIP LIEF GROUP, INC.

Principal Writer and Researcher: Suzanne LeVert

Project Editor: Gary M. Sunshine
Production Coordinator: Laura-Ann Robb
Design Consultants: Emma Crawford, H. Nolan
Photographic Research: Diane Hamilton
Additional Photography: Michael Campbell
Additional Writing and Research: Sharon Henderson
Additional Research: Anne Pierce
Editorial Assistants: Kelli Daley, Jennifer Hirshlag,
    James Hurley, Midge Smith
Typesetting: Crane Typesetting Service, Inc.

THE AMERICAN CIVIL WAR
A Multicultural Encyclopedia

by The Civil War Society

Volume 5:
Medical Care–Prison Life

Grolier Educational Corporation
Danbury, Connecticut

5580626

Published 1994 by
Grolier Educational Corporation
Danbury, Connecticut 06816

Published by arrangement with
The Philip Lief Group, Inc.
6 West 20th Street
New York, New York 10011

The Civil War Society gratefully acknowledges the National Archives in Washington, D.C., for making available photographs appearing on pages 9, 15, 60, 113, 118, 155, 277, 148, 311, 315, 322, 339, 348, 375, 384, 401, 404, 408, 432, 437, 447, 449, 455, 485, 489, 503, 507, 515, 539, 542, 560, 568, 604, 654, 697, 714.

All other photographs appear courtesy of the Library of Congress in Washington, D.C.

First Edition

ISBN:
Set: 0-7172-7348-2
Volume 1: 0-7172-7341-5
Volume 2: 0-7172-7342-3
Volume 3: 0-7172-7343-1
Volume 4: 0-7172-7344-X
Volume 5: 0-7172-7345-8
Volume 6: 0-7172-7346-6
Volume 7: 0-7172-7347-4

Cataloging information to be obtained directly from Grolier Educational Corporation.

Printed in the United States of America

Contents

A Land Divided : 1861-1865

Union ☐ Confederate ▨ Border States ▨

Introduction

"A house divided against itself cannot stand," declared Abraham Lincoln. In 1861, civil war split our ethnically diverse, philosophically divided country into two warring bodies. Four years and 800,000 deaths later, America stood reunited under one flag.

The American Civil War: A Multicultural Encyclopedia explores this dark and fascinating period in United States history. Suitable for reading, research, and independent study, this vividly illustrated encyclopedia contains 300 entries describing important concepts, dynamic figures, significant places and events, and major battles. Woven into the accounts of famous heroes and military clashes are stories of African-Americans and Native Americans, women, and people of many different ethnic groups. Research into these traditionally ignored areas is crucial to understanding how diverse the people and concerns of the Civil War actually were.

This encyclopedia illustrates the ethnic composition of the country at wartime and will show you what life was like for various ethnic groups. Among those groups represented are African-, French-, Irish-, Italian-, Jewish-, Mormon-, Native, and Scandinavian-Americans. Also featured are individual entries on people and groups of various heritage, like Judah Benjamin, a Jewish member of the Confederate cabinet; and the Garibaldi Guard, a colorfully uniformed regiment entirely comprised of Italian-Americans from New York.

The encyclopedia surveys the most important battles of the war, from the first shots fired on Fort Sumter in South Carolina, through Fredericksburg, Gettysburg, Shiloh, and up to the final cavalry fight at Appomattox Station. The encyclopedia features entries on military leaders like the legendary generals Robert E. Lee, Thomas "Stonewall" Jackson, Ulysses S. Grant, and Philip Sheridan. Politicians appear throughout, including Charles Francis Adams, who served as the U.S. minister to Great Britain during the war, and Alexander Stephens, the vice-president of the Confederate States of America. Individual African-Americans played crucial roles in the war; the encyclopedia explores what happened when Dred Scot sued for his freedom, and how former slaves like Frederick Douglass fought to emancipate all American blacks.

By the mid-nineteenth century, American women were just beginning to gain independence and work outside the home. The stories of women are told throughout the encyclopedia, which details the contributions of Mary Ann "Mother" Bickerdyke, who took medical supplies to the Union front lines; Belle Boyd, a daring Confederate spy; and Harriet Tubman, who helped hundreds of slaves escape to the north via the Underground Railroad.

Information on family life explains the many difficulties civilians endured on the homefront, from the psychological effects of losing a loved one to the scarcity of supplies caused by the Union blockade of Southern ports; an entry on Southern diarist Mary Chesnut provides a firsthand account of the particular hardships felt by Southerners, who watched as the majority of battles were fought on their own territory. An essay on camp life details the day-to-day travails of a Civil War soldier, while entries on medical care and prison life highlight the often unlivable conditions awaiting soldiers off the battlefield.

For convenient research, the encyclopedia is arranged in alphabetical order, by last names of people, battle names, concepts, places, and events. Many of the entries contain cross-references to essays concerning people, events, and ideas that contribute to the reader's understanding of that subject; these references are shown in small capital letters. You will thus be able to look up the subjects referred to and piece together various components of Civil War history.

The last volume of the encyclopedia contains a full index, with page references to each time an important name, event, concept, or battle appears in the text. For additional reading, consult the sources and further reading lists.

A close study of the Civil War will reveal the many different economic, moral, social and cultural forces that shaped the period, and better enable today's student to understand and confront the issues facing our diverse society today.

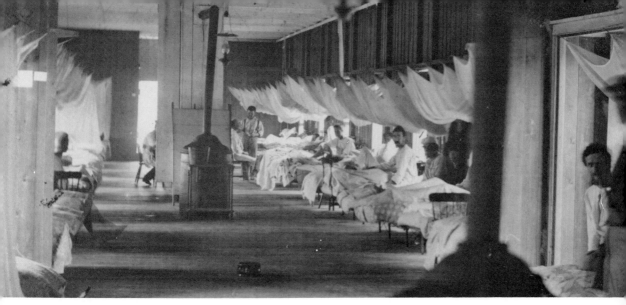

Wards like this one at Harewood Hospital in Washington, D.C. were filled with wounded and diseased soldiers.

Medical Care, Battle Wounds and Disease

The Civil War was fought, claimed the Union army surgeon general, "at the end of the medical Middle Ages." Little was known about what caused disease, how to stop it from spreading, or how to cure it. Surgical techniques ranged from the barbaric to the barely competent.

A Civil War soldier's chances of not surviving the war was about one in four. These fallen men were cared for by a woefully underqualified, understaffed, and undersupplied medical corps. Working against incredible odds, however, the medical corps increased in size, improved its techniques, and gained a greater understanding of medicine and disease every year the war was fought.

During the period just before the Civil War, a physician received minimal training. Nearly all the older doctors served as apprentices in lieu of formal education. Even those who had attended one of the few medical schools were poorly trained. In Europe, four-year medical schools were common, laboratory training was widespread, and a greater understanding of disease and infection existed. The average medical student in the United States, on the other hand, trained for two years or less,

Ambulance wagons and drivers.

received practically no clinical experience, and was given virtually no laboratory instruction. Harvard University, for instance, did not own a single stethoscope or microscope until after the war.

When the war began, the Federal army had a total of about 98 medical officers, the Confederacy just 24. By 1865, some 13,000 Union doctors had served in the field and in the hospitals; in the Confederacy, about 4,000 medical officers and an unknown number of volunteers treated war casualties. In both the North and South, these men were assisted by thousands of women who donated their time and energy to help the wounded. It is estimated that more than 4,000 women served as nurses in Union hospitals; Confederate women contributed much to the effort as well (see SANITARY COMMISSION).

Although Civil War doctors were commonly referred to as "butchers" by their patients and the press, they managed to treat more than 10 million cases of injury and illness in just 48 months and most did it with as much compassion and competency as possible. Poet WALT WHITMAN, who served as a volunteer in Union army hospitals, had great respect for the hard-working physicians, claiming that "All but a few are excellent men. . . ."

Approximately 620,000 men— 360,000 Northerners and 260,000 Southerners—died in the four-year conflict, a figure that tops the total fatalities of all other wars in which America has fought. Of these numbers, approximately 110,000 Union and 94,000 Confederate men died of wounds received in battle. Every effort was made to treat wounded men within 48 hours; most primary care was administered at field hospitals located far behind the front lines. Those who survived were then transported by unreliable and overcrowded ambulances—two-wheeled carts or four-wheeled wagons—to army hospitals located in nearby cities and towns.

The most common Civil War SMALL ARMS ammunition was the dreadful MINIE BALL, which tore an enormous wound on impact: it was so heavy that an abdominal or head wound was almost always fatal, and a hit to an extremity usually shattered any bone encountered. In addition, bullets carried dirt and germs into the wound that often caused infection.

Of the approximately 175,000 wounds to the extremities received among Federal troops, about 30,000 led to amputation; roughly the same proportion occurred in the Confederacy. One witness described a common surgeon's tent this way: "Tables about breast high had been erected upon which the screaming victims were having legs and arms cut off. The surgeons and their assistants, stripped to the waist and bespattered with blood, stood around, some holding the poor fellows while others, armed with long, bloody knives and saws, cut and sawed away with frightful rapidity, throwing the mangled limbs on a pile nearby as soon as removed."

Contrary to popular myth, most amputees did not experience the surgery without anesthetic. Ample doses of chloroform were administered beforehand; the screams heard were usually from soldiers just informed that they would lose a limb or who were witness to the plight of other soldiers under the knife.

Those who survived their wounds and surgeries still had another hurdle, however: the high risk of infection. While most surgeons were aware of a relationship between cleanliness and low infection rates, they did not know how to sterilize their equipment. Due to a frequent shortage of water, surgeons often went days without washing their hands or instruments, thereby passing germs from one patient to another as he treated them. The resulting vicious infections, commonly known as "surgical fevers," are believed to have been caused largely by *Staphylococcus aureus* and *Streptococcus pyogenes*, bacterial cells which generate pus, destroy tissue, and release deadly toxins into the bloodstream. Gangrene, the rotting away of flesh caused by the obstruction of blood flow, was also common after surgery. Despite these fearful odds, nearly 75 percent of the amputees survived.

While the average soldier believed the bullet was his most nefarious foe, disease was the biggest killer of the war. Of the Federal dead, roughly three out of five died of disease, and of the Confederate, perhaps two out of three. One of the reasons for the high rates of disease was the slipshod recruiting process that allowed under- or over-age men and those in noticeably poor health to join the armies on both sides, especially in the first year of the war. In fact, by late 1862, some 200,000 recruits originally accepted for service were judged physically unfit and discharged, either because they had fallen ill or because a routine examination revealed their frail condition.

About half of the deaths from disease during the Civil War were caused by intestinal disorders, mainly typhoid fever, diarrhea, and dysentery. The remainder died from pneumonia and tuberculosis. Camps populated by young soldiers who had never before been exposed to a large variety of common contagious diseases were plagued by outbreaks of measles, chickenpox, mumps, and whooping cough.

The culprit in most cases of wartime illness, however, was the shocking filth of the army camp itself. An inspector in late 1861 found most Federal camps "littered with refuse, food, and other rubbish, sometimes in an offensive state of decomposition; slops deposited in pits within the camp limits or thrown out of broadcast; heaps of manure and offal close to the camp." As a result, bacteria and viruses spread through the camp like wildfire. Bowel disorders constituted the soldiers' most common complaint. The Union army reported that more than 995 out of every 1,000 men eventually contracted chronic diarrhea or dysentery during the war; the Confederates fared no better.

Typhoid fever was even more devastating. Perhaps one-quarter of noncombat deaths in the Confederacy resulted from this disease, caused by the consumption of food or water contaminated by *salmonella* bacteria. Epidemics of malaria spread through camps located next to stagnant swamps teeming with *anopheles* mosquito. Although treatment with quinine reduced fatalities, malaria nevertheless struck approximately one quarter of all servicemen; the Union army alone reported one million cases of it during the course of the war. Poor diet and exposure to the elements only added to the burden (see CAMP LIFE). A simple cold often developed into pneumonia, which was the third leading killer disease of the war, after typhoid and dysentery.

Throughout the war, both the South and the North struggled to improve the level of medical care given to their men. In many ways, their efforts assisted in the birth of modern medicine in the United States. More complete records on medical and surgical activities were kept during the war than ever before, doctors became more adept at surgery and at the use of anesthesia, and

perhaps most importantly, a greater understanding of the relationship between cleanliness, diet, and disease was gained not only by the medical establishment but by the public at large. Another important advance took place in the field of nursing, where respect for the role of women in medicine rose considerably among both doctors and patients (see CLARA BARTON; MARY EDWARDS WALKER).

Meigs, Montgomery

1816–1892

In his largely thankless but critical position as Union quartermaster general, Meigs kept the Federal army astonishingly well supplied throughout the four years of the Civil War. The Georgia native and West Point graduate had earlier served in the army engineering corps, where he supervised construction on the U.S. Capitol building—including its dome and Senate and House wings—as well as Washington's Potomac aqueduct.

When the war began, Meigs remained with the Union army and in June 1861 was appointed

to his quartermaster general post, replacing fellow Southerner JOSEPH E. JOHNSTON, who had resigned to become a major figure in the Confederacy. Meigs' task in his new position was a daunting one: to provide all the non-food, non-weapon supplies for a two-million man military force fighting an epic war of invasion. Uniforms and shoes, tents and blankets, horses and wagons, to name just a few; the quartermaster general had not only to obtain all these items, but to store them and then have them transported to Union forces often hundreds of miles away.

Responsible for the transportation of troops as well, Meigs, in one logistical coup, assembled a flotilla of 400 vessels that carried the entire ARMY OF THE POTOMAC—120,000 men and their equipment—to Fortress Monroe, Virginia, in March 1862 for the beginning of General GEORGE MCCLELLAN's ill-fated PENINSULA CAMPAIGN. Meigs' peacetime engineering experience equipped him well for dealing with military contractors, as he instituted an effective program of

Quartermaster General Montgomery Meigs

competitive bidding to keep costs down. An extremely efficient man, he was also able to reduce substantially the corruption and waste attending the acquisition of over $1.5 billion worth of wartime supplies.

Continuing to mourn the loss of his soldier son in 1864, believed to have been killed by Confederate guerrillas, Meigs remained quartermaster general until his retirement in 1882.

Mexican War

1846–1848

This two-year war over 525,000 square miles of territory laid the groundwork for the Civil War in several respects. First, Texas, the largest acquisition of land since the Louisiana Purchase, revived the nation's political and moral debate over SLAVERY. Second, the battlefields of Mexico proved excellent training ground for many soldiers and generals who would later fight in the Civil War.

The roots of the Mexican War date back to the early 1820s, when the Mexican government granted permission to Stephen Austin, an American citizen, to

settle its sparsely populated northern territories. Within a decade, more than 30,000 Americans—many of them slave owners—called the territory home, outnumbering Mexican residents four to one.

The Mexican government attempted to regain control of the land by enacting laws that abolished slavery and controlled the number of weapons brought in by the Americans. These and other invasive measures were met with an armed insurrection led by Sam Houston, an American frontiersman and politician. After the settlers won a decisive victory at San Jacinto on April 26, 1836, the Mexican government agreed to grant independence to the new Republic of Texas. The size of the territory was in dispute, however, with Texas claiming the Rio Grande as its southwestern border and the Mexicans limiting it to the Nueces River.

For about three years, the future of the new republic remained unsettled. In the United States, Southerners saw its acquisition as a way to gain

Ulysses S. Grant leading his men toward victory at the City of Mexico.

the upper hand in the ongoing fight with Northern states for political power: below the 36° 30″ parallel designated as the boundary for slavery in the MISSOURI COMPROMISE and with slaveholders already residing in the territory, Texas would certainly come into the Union as a slave state.

Equally important was a growing sense of "manifest destiny," the feeling among many Americans that the country had a kind of divine right to expand its territory on the continent. President James Polk, a Southerner from Virginia, attained congressional approval for the annexation of Texas on March 1, 1845; it was formally admitted into the Union on December 29, 1845. In the meantime, Polk attempted to secure the disputed territory for the United States as well as acquire additional land (California and New Mexico) from the Mexican government. In November 1845, he sent an emissary to Mexico City with an offer to purchase the new land for about $30 million, an offer that was immediately rejected.

Relations between the two countries continued to deteriorate. Matters were brought

General Scott entering Mexico.

to a head when Polk ordered Major General Zachary Taylor, who was stationed with about 4,000 men on the Nueces River, to advance to the Rio Grande. Taylor reached the river in April 1846. On April 25, a party of Mexican soldiers surprised and defeated American cavalry just north of the Rio Grande. The news of the battle provoked Congress to declare war on Mexico on May 13, 1846.

The ensuing conflict pitched a well-equipped, well-trained but relatively small American army against large numbers of underfed, poorly armed Mexicans. Although in unfamiliar territory and greatly outnumbered in nearly every battle, American forces under Taylor and, in 1847, General Winfield Scott, eventually out-fought their spirited opponents led by the indomitable president of Mexico, Antonio López de Santa Anna. Thousands of American soldiers who later fought on both sides of the Civil War participated in the conquest, including ULYSSES S. GRANT, WILLIAM T. SHERMAN, GEORGE B. MCCLELLAN, GEORGE MEADE, ROBERT E. LEE, THOMAS "STONEWALL" JACKSON, and Confederate President JEFFERSON DAVIS.

The Mexican War ended after American forces, victorious at the fierce battle of Chapultepec, occupied Mexico City on September 14, 1847. For months, however, the Mexican government refused to negotiate a peace treaty until a new president ready to compromise replaced the intransigent Santa Anna. On February 2, 1848, the Treaty of Guadalupe Hidalgo ceded to the United States more than 525,000 square miles of territory, which would eventually comprise the states of California, Nevada, and Utah, most of Arizona, and New Mexico, and parts of Colorado and Wyoming.

The question of whether these territories would become slave or free states caused great controversy in the U.S. Congress. The South believed its survival was, in part, contingent upon the spread of slavery throughout the West; without this proliferation, the South would find itself at the mercy of Northern senators. The issue was resolved, however temporarily, with the COMPROMISE OF 1850.

Minié Ball

The development of this half-inch lead rifle bullet revolutionized warfare, while the slowness of Civil War military leaders to adapt their tactics to adjust to the new technology was greatly responsible for the overwhelming number of battlefield deaths.

Before the introduction of what soldiers commonly called the "minnie ball"—even though it was indeed bullet-shaped—the use of rifles in battle was impractical and largely limited to corps of elite marksmen. Expensive, tight-fitting projectiles had to be jammed into the grooves of the rifle's muzzle, a time-consuming process.

In 1848, however, French army Captain Claude F. Minié created a smaller, hollow-based bullet that could far more quickly and easily be rammed into the bore, expanding when the weapon was fired to catch in the rifling and be

The minié ball greatly increased the fighting power of the individual soldier.

shot spinning out of the barrel. That spin made the minié ball, like other, more expensive and unwieldy rifle bullets, a highly precise and far-traveling projectile. They could reach half-a-mile or more, and an average soldier could easily hit a target 250 yards away.

By 1855, HARPERS FERRY Armory worker James H. Burton had honed an even cheaper

Rifle use was revolutionized by the minié ball.

version of the minié ball, which, along with the rifle itself, soon became widely used in the U.S. Army. It was the standard bullet for both sides in the Civil War, although neither anticipated the enormous difference this would make on the battlefield. Against a defensive line using musket fire—requiring a 25-second reloading period and accurate to only 50 feet or less—a frontal infantry charge was likely to be successful if the assaulting force moved quickly enough.

The widespread use of the minié bullet, however, shifted the balance greatly to the defense's favor. Nevertheless, Civil War generals continued ordering such attacks, learning only after hard and bloody battlefield experience—from the assault on Marye's Heights at FREDERICKSBURG to PICKETT'S CHARGE at GETTYSBURG—that their strategy would have to be altered.

Missionary Ridge, Battle of

NOVEMBER 25, 1863

The Battle of Missionary Ridge is actually the third action to take place in what is generally referred to as the CHATTANOOGA CAMPAIGN, covering three days from November 23 through 25.

As a result of General WILLIAM T. SHERMAN's activity toward the end of the second day in the Battle of Lookout Mountain, Confederate forces under command of Generals BRAXTON BRAGG and Patrick Cleburne became aware of a major Union thrust against their lines on Missionary Ridge near the Tennessee River, with their objective being Tunnel Hill, the site of an old railway tunnel. On the morning of the twenty-fifth, General ULYSSES S. GRANT ordered a three-pronged attack: Sherman would assault Missionary Ridge directly, covered by GEORGE THOMAS' attack at the center. JOSEPH HOOKER would come down from Lookout Mountain and attack the Confederate rear, either preventing the defenders from retreat into Georgia, or pursuing them if they managed to slip away.

The Confederates were fewer in number, owing to the necessity of reinforcing JAMES LONGSTREET's siege of Knoxville, but they held a strong position where the enemy would essentially have to attack uphill in difficult terrain. The Union attack commenced within moments of sunrise, but Cleburne's men held on so tenaciously that by noon there had been no significant gain for Sherman's forces. Hooker's attack was complicated by the Confederates having burned the railroad bridge that would have made the Union assault much easier; he was unable to move troops up onto Missionary Ridge until quite late in the afternoon.

In the center, Thomas discovered the Confederates were entrenched in two positions: at the foot of the ridge, and higher up above the ravines. Under orders from Grant, he made a gallant assault with four full divisions, which overran the lower Confederate positions. As the Federals continued to charge the remaining distance up the slope, Cleburne's men were afraid to fire lest they kill their own comrades below. The Confederate line became severed in numerous places, and Bragg reluctantly ordered a retreat toward CHICKAMAUGA Creek. The divisions of Cleburne and WILLIAM HARDEE covered the retreat, enabling the majority of Bragg's command to cross the Chickamauga in safety. Chattanooga and vicinity were now in Federal control, and Bragg's men departed under the humiliating chanting of the Union soldiers: "Chickamauga! Chickamauga!" in reference to the sound trouncing the Confederates had handed out in September.

Missouri Compromise

1820

For more than three decades following the ratification of the U.S. Constitution in 1783, the issue of SLAVERY remained largely uncontroversial. The Northwest Ordinance, enacted in 1787, provided that all territories north of the Ohio River were to be free and those south were to be slave; so far, the process of settlement and organization had proceeded smoothly.

Following the Louisiana Purchase of 1803, the United States expanded quickly into western territory. By 1819, nine new states had been added, bringing the total to 22, of which half were slave and half were free. However, of the land that remained unsettled west of the Mississippi, only Louisiana (which had been admitted as a slave state in 1812) and the Arkansas Territory would allow slavery if the rules outlined in the 1787 ordinance were obeyed.

The first crisis arose in 1819, when Missouri requested admittance to the Union as a slave state. As most of the territory lay above the Ohio River, such an action would require nullification of the Northwest Ordinance. Moreover, it would create an imbalance in the U.S. Senate, with slave states gaining a majority for the first time. Luckily, the newly formed territory of Maine requested admittance—as a free state—at

The ordinance abolishing slavery in Missouri, formally nullifying the Missouri Compromise of 1820.

about the same time.

In an attempt to solve not only the immediate crisis but to provide a framework for coping with the conflicts that could arise as more states were created, members of Congress, led by the brilliant Henry Clay, negotiated the Missouri Compromise.

Broken down into three parts, each of which was voted on and passed separately, the Missouri Compromise succeeded in admitting Missouri as a slave state, admitting Maine as a free state, and nullifying the Northwest Ordinance by redefining the boundaries of slavery from north of the Ohio River to north of the 36° 30′ parallel.

In addition to offering a practical answer to the question of slavery in the territories—which satisfied both sides of the issue for three decades—the Missouri Compromise implicitly gave to the federal government the power to decide such issues, a power many people did not agree it had. "To compromise," wrote North Carolina Senator Nathaniel Macon, "is to acknowledge the right of Congress to interfere and to legislate on the subject [of slavery], this would be acknowledging too much." Indeed, in many ways, the balance of power between individual states and the federal government would become as important in the development of the Civil War as the question of slavery itself. (See STATES' RIGHTS, COMPROMISE OF 1850)

Mobile Bay, Battle of

AUGUST 5, 1864

This naval engagement determined the fate of the Confederacy's last major open Gulf port east of Texas. While the Union blockade was in place elsewhere, Alabama's Mobile Bay became a center for the receipt of critically needed provisions smuggled into the South from Europe. U.S. Rear Admiral DAVID G. FARRAGUT wanted to try taking the port after he captured NEW ORLEANS in April 1862, but he was not able to begin his preparations until January 1864.

After more than half a year of planning, Farragut's fleet of 14 wooden ships and four IRONCLADS began its attack shortly after dawn on August 5, entering the bay's heavily mined main channel at 6 A.M., with the monitors in front. The Confederates started firing as the Union boats approached the bay's main defense, Fort Morgan. Leading a flotilla of three small, wooden gunboats and the CSS *Tennessee*—the South's largest ironclad—Confederate Admiral Franklin Buchanan commanded the defensive naval forces against an attack for which he had prepared for two years.

Farragut had himself lashed to the mast of his flagship, the *Hartford*, so he could better direct his forces, and watched as his lead ironclad, the *Tecumseh*, struck a mine. Blown out of the

Confederate Fort Morgan at Mobile Bay.

water, the ship sank in minutes with most of its crew. The Federal fleet halted in alarm as the firing continued from Fort Morgan, until Farragut's famous command, "Damn the torpedoes! Full speed ahead." Moving the *Hartford* in front, the Union admiral led his fleet through the minefield with no additional sinkings and past the fort into the bay.

The *Tennessee*, with Buchanan aboard, attempted to ram the Union ships, then traded fire with the vessels before taking refuge at Fort Morgan. While the Union crews began taking the opportunity to have some breakfast, Buchanan pulled the *Tennessee* out from the fort for another attack. The Confederate ironclad, imposing but unwieldy, was quickly surrounded by Federal boats and fired on and rammed repeatedly. Soon adrift and helpless, with commander Buchanan himself seriously wounded, the *Tennessee* surrendered at approximately 10 A.M., and the battle was over.

Union forces, which totaled nearly 3,000, suffered 319 casualties; of the 470 Confederates engaged, there were 312 casualties, most taken as prisoner. The Union navy now effectively controlled Mobile Bay for the remainder of the war, although Fort Morgan was not captured until August 23, and the city of Mobile itself, 30 miles to the north, remained in Confederate control until the following April—three days, in fact, after Lee surrendered.

Molly Maguires

The "Molly Maguires" was a group secretly formed in Ireland in the 1840s for the purpose of halting evictions by frightening landlords' agents; the name derives from the fact that they sometimes disguised themselves as women. In the United States, they were largely a postwar phenomenon, rising out of the mistreatment and prejudice encountered by Irish immigrants in the North. Union veterans returning home in 1865 expected a hero's welcome, but in fact received the cold shoulder from prospective employers, were denied housing, and were treated ill on account of their religion. A group of miners in Pennsylvania, angered by unsafe, unsanitary working conditions, unfair hiring practices, and prejudice directed at Irish people in any manner, modeled themselves on the Maguires from Ireland and took whatever action they thought was appropriate to balance things out and seek reform. Many times these were peaceful actions, like strikes, petitions, and walkouts; however, just as often the actions took a turn toward the violent, involving riots, arson, and

The USS Monitor *and the* CSS Merrimack *(renamed the* CSS Virginia*) at war.*

destruction of property. The movement was an unexpected outgrowth of the confused years right after the war, when Northern veterans who had begun to feel a sense of worth and independence returned home to discover things had not changed much at all. (See IRISH-AMERICANS IN THE CIVIL WAR)

Monitor vs. the *Merrimack* (CSS *Virginia*)

MARCH 8, 1862

Ushering in a revolution in sea combat, the single, inconclusive March 1862 encounter between the Union and the Confederacy's first IRONCLADS was perhaps the most sensational naval battle of the Civil War.

The *Merrimack* (sometimes spelled without the "k") had been one of the U.S. Navy's finest wood steam frigates before Northern forces scuttled it when they were forced to abandon the Norfolk shipyards one week after the fall of FORT SUMTER. Salvaging the wreck in the summer of 1861, Confederate engineers bolted 2- to 4-inch-thick armor plates on the hull and deck, constructed casemate ports for ten guns, and fitted a cast-iron ram to the prow. Most of the peculiar-looking vessel was submerged, with the exposed portion sloped on a 35 degree angle to increase the chances that enemy shells would simply ricochet off its sides. Slow and unwieldy, too unseaworthy for ocean service yet with too deep a draft for shallow rivers, it was still a fearsome craft that could outmatch any wooden ship that came against it.

Reports of the refashioned *Merrimack*, renamed the CSS *Virginia*, drifted north and compelled the Union navy to hasten its own efforts at building an ironclad. The renowned Swedish-American inventor, John Ericsson, who had been tinkering with armored vessel designs for 20 years, developed a unique new ship for the North, protected by four and one half inches of iron plating, with two guns mounted on an innovative revolving turret. Smaller, swifter, and more maneuverable than the *Merrimack*, the *Monitor*, also mostly submerged, was an even odder-looking vessel, described as resembling a "cheesebox on a raft."

Construction was completed in a remarkable 101 days, beating the South's ironclad to the launching slip, and on March 4, 1862, the *Monitor* was towed out of Brooklyn, New York, to join the Federal blockading squadrons off the Carolina coast.

The CSS *Virginia* (though it often remains better known by its former name), was launched at Norfolk Shipyard on March 5. Its crew thinking they were on a trial run, the Confederate ship headed right for battle at HAMPTON ROADS, Virginia, a channel off Newport News at the entrance of the Chesapeake Bay that was a major Union blockading base.

At about 1 P.M. on March 8, the *Virginia* confronted a fleet of five wooden Federal ships. Enemy broadsides bounced off the ironclad as it rammed and sank the *Cumberland*, the Union's mightiest frigate, ran aground and burned the 50-gun *Congress*, and incapacitated the huge flagship *Minnesota* before withdrawing for the night. The Union navy would not suffer such great losses again until the World War II attack on Pearl Harbor. Though its ram had broken off in the fighting and its captain, Franklin Buchanan, had been wounded, the *Virginia* was little damaged, poised to destroy the rest of the Hampton Roads fleet and then to go on and threaten the entire Union blockade.

The *Monitor*'s hasty arrival in the channel at 1 A.M. on March 9 did not initially calm the mounting panic in Washington, D.C. Nearly sinking on its voyage south, the Union vessel seemed barely able to float, let alone fight. But in battle, the *Monitor* proved an equal match to the *Virginia*. Only 100 yards apart, the two ironclads began a furious four-hour duel at 9 A.M. that morning, pounding out artillery fire that scarcely made a dent and colliding several times, both accidentally and in unsuccessful attempts to ram each other. Neither ship could gain the advantage, and when the *Monitor* pulled back after its captain, John L. Worden, was temporarily blinded by a shell blast, the *Virginia*, beginning to leak and have engine problems, withdrew.

The first battle in history between ironclads ended in a draw, though the Union blockade at Hampton Roads held and the North's fears of losing its naval superiority were allayed. Still, the Confederacy proved it could mount a formidable challenge to the Union fleet, as both sides acknowledged the obvious superiority of armored ships and hurried to build more.

The *Monitor* and the *Virginia*, however, never confronted each other again—neither, in fact, remained afloat for long. On May 11, little more than two months after the *Virginia* was launched, the Confederates blew up their pioneer ironclad in Norfolk harbor to prevent its seizure by Union forces that had captured the port. And on December 31, the *Monitor* sank in a storm off the coast of Cape Hatteras, North Carolina.

Morgan's Raids

OCTOBER 1862–JULY 1863

Confederate Brigadier General John Hunt Morgan's three spectacular cavalry raids in Kentucky and Tennessee so disrupted the Union army in the west that President ABRAHAM LINCOLN himself sent an urgent missive to commander HENRY W. HALLECK: "They are having a stampede in Kentucky. Please look to it."

John Hunt Morgan—the epitome of a cavalry commander sitting straight, tall, and fearless in the saddle—had served in the MEXICAN WAR but otherwise had no professional military training.

Brigadier General John H. Morgan

He began his Civil War service as captain, incorporating the Lexington Rifles, a local militia he had organized in 1857, into the Confederate effort when the war began. By the end of 1862, he had been made a brigadier general in command of the 2nd Kentucky Cavalry and was serving under Major General JOSEPH WHEELER in the western theater.

Morgan's first raid undermined Union Major General DON CARLOS BUELL's attempts to capture Chattanooga, Tennessee. From July 4 to August 1, 1862, he and his men covered more than 1,000 miles, captured more than 1,200 prisoners, and destroyed several Union supply depots along the way. Morgan himself lost just 100 men.

Three months later, after serving under General BRAXTON BRAGG during his Kentucky campaign, the clever horseman and his unit joined Lieutenant General Kirby Smith as he attempted to retreat from Kentucky while under fire from pursuing Union troops. With 1,800 men, he circled eastward, captured Lexington, Kentucky, and destroyed Union transportation and communication lines before returning to Tennessee at the beginning of November.

Morgan's third raid, also known as his "Christmas Raid," was designed to help Bragg counter Union Major General William S. Rosecrans' advance through Tennessee. After organizing a division of two brigades totalling about 4,000 men, Morgan headed north from Alexandria, Tennessee, on December 21, 1862, to raid Rosecrans' lines of communication and supply.

Riding through Glasgow and Bardstown, he reached the Louisville & Nashville Railroad and followed it to Rolling Fork, near Elizabethtown, capturing the town and severing Rosecrans' lines.

By this time, the Union army had tracked the cavalrymen and were preparing to attack them as they headed back to Confederate lines. Morgan, realizing the danger, made his escape during the night with minimal loss of life, returning to camp on January 2, 1863. In just over a week, he and his men managed to destroy more than two million dollars worth of Union property and capture about 1,900 troops.

Morgan's final raid took place during July 1863. While his commander, Braxton Bragg, had directed him merely to slow Rosecrans' advance on CHATTANOOGA, Morgan instead invaded Ohio. He hoped that a show of Confederate strength would raise support for the Southern cause among Yankees who were both tired of the war and sympathetic in some manner to the South. Although he did inflict damage on the Union supply lines, this raid appeared to more like a reckless adventure than a well-planned offensive.

On July 2, Morgan managed to elude more than 10,000 Union troops and took about 2,500 men across the Cumberland River. Wreaking his usual havoc on his way north, he joined in several skirmishes with Federals while completing the longest continuous march of the war, covering 90 miles in just 35 hours.

On the afternoon of July 13, he arrived in Harrison, Ohio, with a reduced force of 2,000 and with the Union already planning his capture. Indeed, his men had already captured 6,000 men, mobilized thousands of Union troops, destroyed 25 bridges, and demolished scores of railroads. By July 18, however, Morgan began to encounter serious enemy action; the next day, he was badly beaten by forces under Union Brigadier General Edward H. Hobson at Buffington Island. Supported by militia and gunboats, the Union troops managed to devastate Morgan's crew, killing about 120 and capturing another 700.

Morgan himself managed to escape with about 300 men and made a desperate effort to reach Pennsylvania. Hobson pursued relentlessly, finally capturing the wily horseman on July 26, at

New Lisbon. Morgan and his raiders were then imprisoned in the Ohio State Penitentiary. Remarkably, Morgan was able to escape, although he was killed just about a month later during a cavalry encounter at Greeneville, Tennessee, on September 3, 1864.

Mormons in the Civil War

The Mormons, a religious group living primarily in the American West around Utah at the time of the Civil War, were not actively involved in the SECESSION crisis back East. Having come out of what they considered to be the "sinful, fleshly world" to follow their charismatic young leaders Joseph Smith and Brigham Young, the Mormons established what they hoped would be a New Jerusalem in a land set aside for them by God. They believed that the Native Americans were the lost tribe of Israel and moved west to be with them. At this time in their development the Mormons practiced polygamy, the taking of more than one wife in marriage. They believed such marriages were legally binding, though the territorial law of the United States did not agree.

By coincidence, the Mormons provided an opportunity for the up and coming young men of the U.S. Army to practice for what would become the all encompassing Civil War. Between 1857 and 1860, the Mormons were the focus of a great deal of military activity as a sizeable force under the command of Colonel ALBERT SIDNEY JOHNSTON was sent to prevent Smith's followers from taking control of sections of Nevada and Utah—with every intent of seceding from the Union and forming their own nation. Soldiers whose names would be emblazoned on the annals of the Civil War had to confront many of the same issues they would be dealing with on a national scale very soon: the right of a state or territory to disalign itself from the government if its needs and preferences were not being met or respected; the level to which the government ought to be allowed to gain involvement in the religious, civil and legal customs of a state or territory, and at what point armed intervention can go before the local citizenry exercises the right of self-defense.

Just a small sampling of names from the expedition's rosters is sufficient to indicate the men to whom these formerly abstract concepts became daily reality under fire: Philip St. George Cooke, father-in-law of JEB STUART; G. W. CUSTIS and WILLIAM H. F. "ROONEY" LEE, sons of ROBERT E. LEE; FITZ-JOHN PORTER; Stephen Dill Lee; and JOHN BELL HOOD.

Once these men and their comrades were involved in their own secession war in the East, the Mormons found themselves being left largely alone, save for being under the watchful eye of the few U.S. troops left in the territories during the period of 1861 to 1865. Dedicated to the preservation of their way of life and beliefs, the Mormons passed the ongoing years in peaceful, even friendly relations with the Native American population of their area. They eventually put aside some of the more extreme practices of their faith and distilled Joseph Smith's teachings down to an essential kernel of belief that has sustained them in the twentieth century.

Mosby's Rangers

Numbering about 800 at its greatest strength, this corps of PARTISAN rangers sabotaged Union efforts in northern and western Virginia so successfully that historians believe they prolonged the life of the Confederacy for more than a year.

Formed in December 1862 by Confederate cavalry commander JEB STUART, the Rangers were made up of men on leave from army units, convalescents, and civilians unwilling to enlist in the Confederate army. Leading the men was the clever and fearless John Mosby (1833–1916). A diminutive man of just 125 pounds, Mosby had fought in the cavalry corps at FIRST BULL RUN, then joined Stuart's cavalry as a scout; Mosby originated the idea for Stuart's ride around Major General GEORGE B. MCCLELLAN's Union army during the PENINSULA CAMPAIGN. An impetuous, independent man— he became an attorney by studying for the law while in prison for shooting a fellow student at the University of Virginia—Mosby chafed under strict army rules.

After the Confederate Congress authorized the organization of partisan bands through the 1862

Colonel John S. Mosby

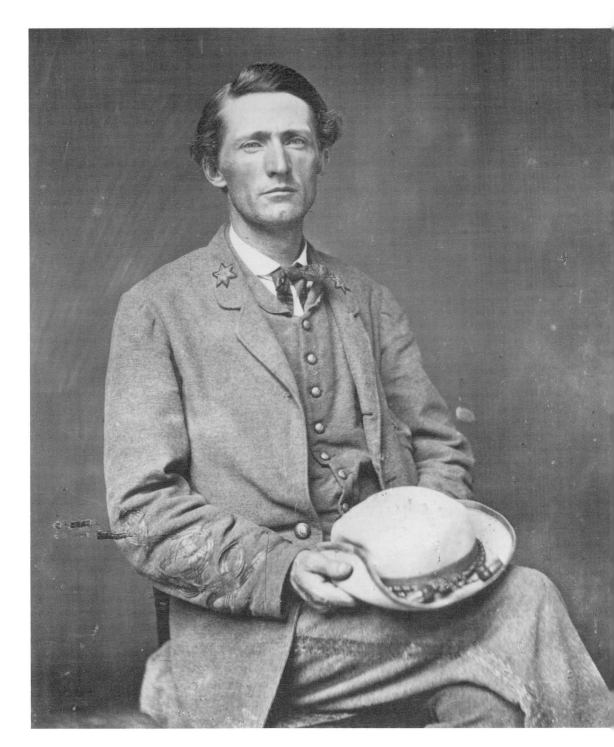

Mosby and his Maryland battalion.

Partisan Ranger Act, Mosby convinced Stuart to give him an independent command. Mosby's Rangers operated from private homes and individual camps in western Virginia and only met as a group when Mosby called them together. Their military techniques were equally unconventional. They usually attacked in small groups in the dead of night, carried Colt .44 revolvers rather than swords or rifles, and more than once kidnapped Union officers and enlisted men after waking them from a sound sleep.

On March 8, 1863, Mosby and 29 of his men managed to capture Brigadier General Edwin Stoughton, two captains, and 30 enlisted men in the middle of the night in Fairfax Court House, Virginia. In addition, they also managed to garner 58 horses from the raid, the loss of which apparently upset Union President ABRAHAM LINCOLN more than the lost personnel. "I can make new brigadier generals," Lincoln remarked, "but I can't make new horses."

For the most part, Mosby's Rangers focused on attacking Union trains and supply depots, destroying them after appropriating their contents. In the summer of 1863, as ROBERT E. LEE made his second invasion of the North after his victory at CHANCELLORSVILLE, Mosby and his men followed, undermining Union efforts to mount an effective counterattack. On June 10, shortly after hearing they had been officially designated the 43rd Battalion of Partisan Rangers, Mosby and his men rode into Maryland and burned a Union camp at Seneca Mills to

Clash between Union soldiers and Mosby's Rangers.

the ground. "Mosby is an old rat and has a great many holes," wrote one of the many Union soldiers trying to put an end to the costly war of attrition Mosby was waging.

By August 1863, at least two prominent cavalry companies— the 2nd Massachusetts and the 13th New York—were ordered to pursue the clever horsemen on a full-time basis, but Mosby's Rangers remained elusive. In fact, just before and during PHILIP HENRY SHERIDAN'S SHENANDOAH VALLEY CAMPAIGN of 1864–1865, the Rangers reached their peak in terms of manpower, activity, and effectiveness. On July 6, 1864, Mosby's guerrillas swooped down upon a camp at Mount Zion Church, killing 40 Union cavalrymen and taking about 60 others prisoner. Their attack several days later at Fairfax Station achieved nearly the same results, as did another outside of Falls Church a few weeks after that. In late summer, Robert E. Lee noted that during the previous six months alone, Mosby and his men had killed, wounded, or captured 1,200 Federals and had taken more than 1,600 horses and mules, 230 head of cattle, and 85 wagons.

During the fall of 1864, Mosby's Rangers continued to wreak havoc by upsetting Union plans to repair the vital Orange & Alexandria rail line at Manassas. The Rangers derailed trains, tore up tracks, and shot construction workers, so terrorizing Union forces that Secretary of War EDWIN STANTON ordered that every house within five miles of the tracks be burned unless its owner was "known to be friendly." The threat was carried out, but the guerrillas continued their activities.

During the fall of 1864, Sheridan ordered Captain Richard Blazer to recruit 100 men and, equipping them with repeating rifles, led them on a search-and-destroy mission against Mosby's band. The "Gray Ghost," as Mosby was known, outmaneuvered Blazer on November 18; during a surprise attack, the Rangers killed or wounded all but two of Blazer's men and captured their weapons.

By the spring of 1865, the clever horsemen controlled a vast stretch of land between the Potomac and the Rappahannock known by friend and enemy alike as "Mosby's Confederacy." Hardly a day went by without a Ranger attack; even after word reached them of Lee's April 9, 1865, surrender at APPOMATTOX COURT HOUSE, they continued to fight in the mountains.

After General JOSEPH E. JOHNSTON's surrender about two weeks later, however, Mosby called his partisans together and urged them to surrender. Mosby, who had been wounded seven times during the course of the war, returned to Warrenton, Virginia, and practiced law until his death on May 30, 1916.

Mud March

JANUARY 20–23, 1863

ARMY OF THE POTOMAC Commander AMBROSE BURNSIDE led an ill-advised, ill-fated January 1863 attempt to flank ROBERT E. LEE's Confederate forces. After his dreadful defeat the previous month in the Battle of FREDERICKSBURG, Burnside was determined to redeem himself and, in his words, "strike a great

The Mud March, January 21, 1863.

and mortal blow to the rebellion." His troops encamped along the Rappahannock River not far from the battle site, the Union general planned to engage the ARMY OF NORTHERN VIRGINIA, waiting on the opposite bank, in combat once again. Burnside's corps commanders thought the idea was a terrible one and insisted their exhausted and demoralized men needed a rest. Nevertheless, Burnside persisted with his scheme for the entire army to head north, cross the river at Banks' Ford, and attack Lee's left flank.

On the morning of January 20, the march began, auspiciously at first. By mid-afternoon, however, it started to rain—just a drizzle at first, then a freezing, torrential downpour that fell relentlessly for the next three days. The dirt roads became impassable; indeed, they practically became swamps. The drenched army, along with its ARTILLERY, horses, wagons, and pontoons, got hopelessly bogged down in "18 feet of mud," as one officer put it. Some mule teams drowned in the mire.

From across the river, Confederate troops, enjoying the hapless spectacle, jeered at their foes and held up signs mockingly pointing the way to RICHMOND.

Burnside, desperate to raise spirits, issued whiskey to his men, but the ensuing drunkenness only made matters worse. With morale sagging still further, desertion hit a new high. And still the icy rain fell.

Finally, on January 23, Burnside called an end to the fiasco—which became known even in official reports as "the Mud March"—ordering his soaked troops back to camp. Two days later, ABRAHAM LINCOLN removed Burnside from command, and the dispirited Army of the Potomac got the rest it sorely needed.

Murfreesboro, Battle of

DECEMBER 31, 1862–JANUARY 2, 1863

The close of the war's first full year brought action at last on the Tennessee front between Confederate defender BRAXTON BRAGG and his Union opponent William S. Rosecrans. After several days of impending attack, both generals curiously enough came to nearly exact conclusions: it was the last day of the year, they must make some sort of demonstration, and it would be

Sheridan's Union forces at Murfreesboro.

to fling the left extreme of their line against the right flank of the enemy. Bragg, however, put his plan into motion while Rosecrans was still trying to feel his way; just after dawn WILLIAM HARDEE sent his corps smashing into the Union right. This set what would be the Federal standard for the day, as Rosecrans' forces remained essentially on the defensive throughout the fighting.

As each Confederate move was made, a mirror maneuver was enacted on the Union side to attempt to counter it; the Federals fell back to the difficult position of trying to hold the turnpike which ran between Murfreesboro and Nashville, with Stone's River at their back—never a good tactical position in which to find oneself, but worse in the dead of winter with the water high and cold. Constantly under attack from the cavalry under General JOSEPH WHEELER, and knowing he was in a daunting position, Rosecrans ordered the assault abandoned and concentrated his line on the turnpike. The fighting continued without conclusion until well into the afternoon; the Federals held on stubbornly, inflicting heavy casualties on the Confederates.

By the end of the day, the two armies settled in for a long, cold night, each expecting to continue in the morning. In one of the more poignant incidents of the war, a military band on one side began to play "Home, Sweet Home." As the notes sounded across the cold ground that had been a killing field in the daylight, a band on the opposing side joined in to play along in the darkness. In the silence that followed the tune, the two armies caught what little sleep they could almost within sight of one another on the field of battle.

The Confederates used the darkness to entrench; the Federal commanders met in an attempt to design a new strategy. After much discussion, it was decided they would remain and fight it out. Curiously enough, however, as the new day and new year dawned, almost nothing of a military nature occurred; there were occasional sporadic outbreaks of firing, and once or twice a brief artillery duel, but neither army came forward on the muddy ground to offer battle.

It was not until the early morning hours of January 2, 1863, that anything substantive happened—and that turned out to be very gallant, very bloody, and tactically pointless. Confederate JOHN C. BRECKINRIDGE led his men to take a hill to the northeast of Stone's River, which they did with accompanying high casualties, only to be attacked in force and pushed back by superior strength bolstered by a shattering artillery barrage. The two armies did nothing more for the rest of the day, but sat back to contemplate their heavy losses: between wounded, killed or missing, the Federal forces had been depleted by almost 13,000 out of over 40,000; the Confederates suffered nearly 12,000 out of 35,000 men lost or no longer able to fight.

Rebel soldiers of the 9th Mississippi Infantry at Murfreesboro.

There was a brief attack the following day, January 3, as the Federals demonstrated against Bragg's lines near the river, but very little came of it, and there was no return to the general conflict. The Federals were astounded but gratified when, for no reason they could see, Bragg withdrew his forces from Murfreesboro along the Manchester Turnpike for the next day or so. Rosecrans moved his men into the town on January 5, 1863, and was wired by ABRAHAM LINCOLN that he had the admiration and congratulations of his country for the victory. Two weeks later, on January 21, Braxton Bragg discovered what his country thought of him for his curious retreat: President JEFFERSON DAVIS sent General JOSEPH E. JOHNSTON to investigate the Army of Tennessee's commander, looking into reasons

1st Tennessee Colored Battery on its way to Nashville, November 23, 1864.

he had for abandoning Murfreesboro, and to see if there was any substance to criticisms of Bragg that had reached RICHMOND. Bragg would not be relieved of command, but Davis' confidence in him was seriously impaired for a long time to come.

Nashville, Battle of

DECEMBER 15–16, 1864

The Confederate Army of Tennessee under JOHN BELL HOOD was crushed after a two-day onslaught by GEORGE HENRY THOMAS' Union troops outside Nashville in December 1864, a decisive clash that ended the major fighting in the Civil War's western theater.

Fresh from the catastrophic November 30 defeat at Franklin, 75 miles south of the state capital, Hood refused to abandon his quixotic invasion of Tennessee, still irrationally hoping his army could retake the state, collect reinforcements, and mount new assaults on Union forces in Virginia and the Ohio Valley. Also thinking that a retreat would invite large-scale desertion, the undaunted Confederate commander ordered his demoralized troops—one quarter of whom were marching barefoot—forward toward Nashville. There, they faced a

Union force twice as large as their own—Thomas' 30,000 troops, sent earlier by WILLIAM T. SHERMAN to ward off the Confederate advance, joined by John Schofield's equally large army that had just come up from Franklin.

Occupying the Tennessee capital since early 1862, the Union military had already turned the city into a near-impenetrable fortress. By the time Hood's army arrived in the hills a few miles south on December 2, there was little the Confederates could do either to dislodge or pass the enemy. With far too few troops for an effective siege or a direct assault, and unable to advance around the city without exposing their rear and flank, the Southerners dug in and formed a wide defensive line, hoping for reinforcements and waiting for Thomas' attack.

Recognizing his adversary's dire position, the methodical Union commander took his time preparing his army's offensive. Back in Virginia, ULYSSES S. GRANT was livid at the delay. Overestimating Hood and underestimating Thomas, the Union general-in-chief feared that the Army of Tennessee was poised to prolong the nearly concluded war by invading Northern territory and wired several urgent messages to

Union camp awaiting confrontation with C.S.A. Lieutenant General John Bell Hood at Nashville.

Nashville ordering an immediate attack. Thomas ignored the directives as he waited for a heavy sleet storm to pass, while Grant headed to Tennessee to relieve the general and take charge of the operation himself.

Before he arrived, Thomas struck at last. On the morning of December 15, three Union corps began hammering the Confederate left while an ancillary infantry and cavalry attack kept Southern troops busy at the other end of the line. Barely holding on until sundown, Hood's army finally fell back two miles that night to a new defensive position extending between two hills.

Thomas did not know whether the Confederates had retreated altogether in the dark and waited until the following afternoon to mount a renewed assault. Hood's troops were able to repel a charge on Overton Hill to their right, but by 4 P.M. his entire left flank was virtually surrounded by Union infantry, cavalry, and artillery. Smashing suddenly through the line with astonishing force as a hard rain fell, the Northerners utterly routed the Confederate army. Nearly an entire division—cannon and all—was captured as hundreds of Southern troops surrendered, while others abandoned their weapons and supplies to flee more quickly.

Followed closely by Union horsemen, the splintered remnants of the Army of Tennessee continued retreating for the next two weeks all the way to Mississippi, covered in the rear by NATHAN BEDFORD FORREST'S fighting cavalry. For such a conclusive battle, the casualties were surprisingly light—fewer than 400 Federals killed and about 1,500 Confederates killed or wounded. But with its twin defeats at Franklin and Nashville and its subsequent headlong retreat, John Bell Hood's army was demolished.

In January 1865, the general resigned a command that had all but ceased to exist, while most of his surviving troops were sent back into combat in the East to stem Sherman's unstoppable advance through the Carolinas.

Native Americans in the Civil War

Despite decades of scholarship, many misperceptions persist

Chippewa agent, Hole-In-The-Day.

concerning the Civil War. The war is often viewed, for example, as solely a white man's war; it is also often thought to have taken place solely in the East and South. Modern historians are attempting to dispel these notions, both of which serve to obscure the participation of Native Americans in the Civil War.

During the period of 1861 to 1865, Native Americans all over the continent were struggling for autonomy, as peoples with their own organization, culture, and life-style. Some tribes, like the Cherokees, were directly involved in the war. Other Native Americans living in the war-torn areas of the East made individual decisions as to whether they wished to have anything to do with the situation. Still others, living in the mountains, prairies, and deserts of the rest of the country, suddenly realized they had a chance to take back some of their own land, as they saw fewer and fewer U.S. Army soldiers assigned to forts in their tribal areas.

Statistics show that just under 3,600 Native Americans served in the Union Army during the war. Perhaps the best known of their number was Colonel Ely Parker, who served as an aide to General U. S. GRANT, and was present at ROBERT E. LEE's surrender at APPOMATTOX COURT HOUSE. Statistics for the Confederacy are not reliably available, but most scholars of Native American involvement in the actual fighting of the war are very well acquainted with the major Southern figure among them: Brigadier General Chief STAND WATIE, a three-quarter blood Cherokee who was born in December 1806 near what would become Rome, Georgia. Stand Watie was one of the signers of a treaty that agreed to the removal of the Cherokee from their home in Georgia to what was then the Oklahoma territory; this split the tribes into two factions, and Stand Watie became the leader of the minority party.

At the outbreak of the Civil War, the minority party gave its allegiance to the Confederacy, while the majority party went for

Wounded Native American sharpshooters on Mayre's Heights near Fredericksburg.

the North. Watie organized a company, then a regiment known as the First Cherokee Mounted Rifles; the regiment fought at Wilson's Creek, Elkhorn, and in numerous smaller fights and skirmishes along the border with what was known as Indian Territory. The warriors found curious the white man's strategy of standing still and allowing people to shoot at them, or lob ARTILLERY shells at them; the Cherokee tended to be spectacular at wildly brave mounted charges, but once the artillery began to fire, the warriors wanted nothing to do with it. Stand Watie was unreconstructed to the end; it is believed he never surrendered until June 23, 1865, well after other Confederate commanders had given up. He died in 1871 and is buried in the Old Ridge Cemetery in Delaware County, Oklahoma.

While the war was raging back East, out in the West things were seldom quiet or peaceful. Statistics show that nearly 90 engagements were fought by U.S. troops in the West during the war, most of them involving Native American tribespeople. From January to May 1863, there were almost continuous fights in the New Mexico territory, as part of a concerted effort by the Federal government to contain and control the Apache; in the midst of all this, ABRAHAM LINCOLN met with representatives from several major tribes, and informed them he felt they would never attain the prosperity of the white race unless they turned to farming as a way of life.

In July 1864, there was fighting against Native Americans in Minnesota; fighting continued throughout the year in New Mexico, as well. Then in November, on the twenty-ninth, there occurred what some historians have called the first major blot of the so-called Indian Wars: the Sand Creek Massacre. Frightened by raids made by warriors in the area around Denver as a result of a reduced military presence in the West, Colorado settlers asked Colonel J. M. Chivington to punish the raiders. Chivington, with 900 volunteer militiamen, attacked a peaceful village of some five hundred or more Arapaho and Cheyenne natives, killing women and children as well as warriors. In his report, Chivington chillingly stated: "It may perhaps be unnecessary for me to state that I captured no prisoners."

Some of the people escaped, however, and at least one of them was pursued by irony in the years to come: Chief Black Kettle of the Cheyenne survived the massacre at Sand Creek, only to die at the hands of GEORGE ARMSTRONG CUSTER's 7th Cavalry in a second attack on a peaceful village some three years later, at a place called the Washita River.

After the Civil War, the white presence in the West rose to new levels. Numerous financial crises and depressions hit the East after the boom of the war years, and many families chose to move onward in hopes of finding gold, or purchasing cheap land to start a farm. Men unable to find work in the cities joined the army. As the tribal peoples fought to defend their sacred places, hunting grounds, and even their very way of life, they attacked crews building railroads and sought to drive off hunters and gold prospectors. Conflicting views of what ownership of the land meant, as well as numerous other cultural misunderstandings, led to bloodbath after bloodbath; at Little Big Horn and Beecher's Island, the tribes defeated the white man, only to be battered into defeat themselves at places like Wounded Knee. The official army policy was to provide necessities for the tribes during the winter, then to face the reality of fighting the same people when the weather cleared and they wished to change hunting grounds; this policy was known ironically to the common soldier as "feed 'em in winter, fight 'em in summer."

The unofficial government policy, however, was summed up curtly by General PHILIP SHERIDAN, the man who in 1864 stated he would so devastate the Shenandoah Valley, breadbasket of the Confederacy, that a crow flying through it would have to "carry his own rations." Sheridan, appointed to command of one of the major administrative departments of the territories in the years after the war, made the now-infamous statement: "The only good Indian I ever saw was dead." With an attitude such as this, it was only a matter of time and attrition before the Native Americans saw their way of life taken from them—not forever, though, as the descendants of those who fought to save the Way are even today striving to bring back the old knowledge and customs.

USS gunboat Mendota.

Navy

Both the Federal and Confederate navies played crucial roles in the Civil War; the Union BLOCKADE and naval operations in the western theater were at least as important to the Northern victory as its successful land war. Moreover, the technical and strategic advances made by both sides during the period effectively ushered in the era of modern warfare at sea.

When the Civil War began, neither the Union nor the

Confederacy had strong naval capabilities. The Union had just 90 ships, half of which were out of commission. Its 1,500 officers and 75,000 enlisted men were scattered around the globe; more than 10 percent of its officers would resign to join the Confederacy. Another Union loss to the Confederacy near the beginning of the war was the Norfolk Navy Yard on April 20–21, 1861. However, with its vast industrial and financial resources, the Union quickly established a naval force powerful enough to devastate the South.

At the beginning of the war, the Confederate navy consisted of just 10 ships and 15 guns, and it would struggle throughout the war to maintain its ranks at full strength. At the time of the Civil War, the world's navies were just making the transition from sail to steam and from wooden ships to IRONCLADS. To compensate for its dearth of resources, the Confederate navy attempted to appropriate some of these new technologies. The South was the first to build an ironclad, to experiment with submarine technology, and to use torpedoes during battle (at Yorktown, Virginia, May 1862).

Without question, the major naval operation of the war, for both sides, was the Northern blockade of Southern ports. Under orders from U.S. Navy Secretary GIDEON WELLES, the Union concentrated its force along the Southern coast in order to strangle the Confederate government economically. DAVID FARRAGUT's capture of NEW ORLEANS on April 25, 1862, solidified Union control of the seas. In turn, most of the South's scant naval resources were devoted to efforts at circumventing the blockade; in fact, Confederate Secretary of the Navy STEPHEN MALLORY was criticized for spending too much time and money on building BLOCKADE RUNNERS and in conducting raids on Northern shipping, neither of which did much damage to the blockade in the end. In fact, the North's foreign trade actually increased between 1861 and 1865, while the South's barely survived.

Second in importance only to the blockade were U.S. naval operations on the western rivers. With their potent firepower, Union gunboats helped to capture FORT HENRY, FORT DONELSON, and VICKSBURG, thereby providing secure arteries for moving Union men and matériel across an otherwise impenetrable landscape of lowland mire.

The number of successful combined navy-army operations was limited, however, largely due to lack of a proper chain of command and cooperation between the two branches of the service. In addition, naval commanders, convinced of the ironclads' invincibility, often underestimated the need for the army's help to subdue the enemy. By the end of the war, due to its vast technical and industrial advances, the U.S. Navy had become one of the most powerful forces in the world, with more than 600 ships and 50,000 men. (See *H.L. HUNLEY*)

New Orleans, Battle of

APRIL 25, 1862

DAVID FARRAGUT's impressive April 1862 naval victory placed the Confederacy's largest city and most vital port in the hands of the Union. A hundred miles above the mouth of the Mississippi, New Orleans was the gateway to the great river and to the entire deep South, and its capture could almost divide the Confederacy in two. Military actions elsewhere left the city itself lightly defended, dependent on the protection of Forts Jackson and St. Philip, which guarded the river approach 75 miles downstream. But the garrisons were heavily fortified, and a barricade of hulks in the water stalled vessels right in front of their heavy guns.

With Union naval commander David Porter arguing that sustained mortar fire from boats on the river would disable the forts and allow a fleet of ships to pass all the way to New Orleans, preparations were begun for the attempt in early 1862. Army General BENJAMIN BUTLER captured Ship Island near the mouth of the Mississippi, where David Farragut, squadron captain and Porter's adopted brother, gathered 24 wooden sloops and gunboats, along with Porter's 19 mortar schooners. After delays to make the vessels light enough to pass over the many sand bars, Farragut's fleet started ascending the river in April, supported by 15,000 troops under Butler for possible land battle.

Battle of New Orleans.

On April 18, Porter commenced a six-day barrage of cannon fire on the two forts, an incessant bombardment of over 3,000 shells a day that did more to rattle Union crews with the constant pounding than to weaken the Confederate defenses. Perhaps distracted by the shelling, however, the

An angry crowd greets the Union fleet at New Orleans.

Southerners did not seem to notice when two Federal gunboats approached the river barricade on the night of April 20 and cleared a small passageway through. With Porter's bombardment making little impact, Farragut ordered his fleet to proceed anyway. Hidden by the dark, the boats started their audacious run at 2 A.M. on April 24.

Cannon fire from the forts, answered by Union shelling from the river, quickly lit up the sky in a dazzling nighttime fireworks display. Their two nearby ironclads not yet fully operational, the Confederates launched a small squadron of wooden ships to ram the Federal boats and sent rafts set ablaze to impede the advance. Farragut's flagship, the *Hartford*, caught fire and ran aground, but was afloat again shortly as the Union fleet proceeded to sink or disable the enemy vessels. After an hour and a half of pounding battle, all but four of Farragut's boats managed to pass the Confederate forts, despite some heavy damage and nearly 170 men killed or injured.

On April 25, Farragut steamed into New Orleans, defended now only by angry pistol-bearing citizens, and captured the city without further combat, though the mayor refused to formally surrender. Butler's troops arrived on April 29, beginning their harsh occupation, while the day before, Forts Jackson and St. Philip, whose disheartened soldiers had begun to mutiny, surrendered, too.

It was a disastrous defeat for the South. Although the Union did not yet control the entire Mississippi, the entrance to the waterway that bisected the Confederacy and served as its lifeline would remain cut off for the rest of the war.

New York Draft Riots

JULY 11–13, 1863

"The nation is at this time in a state of Revolution, North, South, East and West," wrote the editor of the Washington *Times* during the often violent protests that occurred after ABRAHAM LINCOLN issued the March 3, 1863, Enrollment Act of CONSCRIPTION. Although demonstrations took place in many Northern cities, the riots that broke out in New York City were both the most violent and the most publicized.

With a large and powerful Democratic party operating in the city, a dramatic show of dissent had been long in the making. The state's popular governor, Democrat Horatio Seymour, openly despised Lincoln and his policies. In addition, the Enrollment Act shocked a population already tired of the two-year-old war.

By the time the names of the first draftees were drawn in New York City on July 11, reports about the carnage of GETTYSBURG had been published in city papers. Lincoln's call for 300,000 more young men to fight a seemingly endless war frightened even those who supported the Union cause. Moreover, the Enrollment Act contained several exemptions, including the payment of a "commutation fee" that allowed wealthier and more

In New York, backlash against the draft erupted in riot.

influential citizens to buy their way out of service.

Perhaps no group was more resentful of these inequities than the Irish immigrants populating the slums of northeastern cities. Poor and more than a little prejudiced against blacks—with whom they were both unfamiliar and forced to compete for the lowest-paying jobs—the Irish in New York objected to fighting on their behalf.

On Sunday, June 12, the names of the draftees drawn the day before by the provost marshall were published in newspapers. Within hours, groups of irate citizens, many of them Irish immigrants, banded together across the city. Eventually numbering some 50,000 people, the mob terrorized neighborhoods on the East Side of New York for three days looting scores of stores. Blacks were the targets of most attacks on citizens; several lynchings and beatings occurred. In addition, a black church and orphanage were burned to the ground.

All in all, the mob caused more than $1.5 million of damage. The number killed or wounded during the riot is unknown, but estimates range from two dozen to nearly 100. Eventually, Lincoln deployed combat troops from the Federal ARMY OF THE POTOMAC to restore order; they remained encamped around the city for several weeks. In the end, the draft raised only about 150,000 troops throughout the North, about three-quarters of them substitutes, amounting to just one-fifth of the total Union force.

Northern Virginia, Army of

"There were never such men in an army before. They will go anywhere and do anything if properly led." So claimed ROBERT E. LEE, the commander of the Confederacy's principal field force after leading it to victory at CHANCELLORSVILLE, one of the most brilliantly planned and executed engagements of the war.

Previously called the ARMY OF THE POTOMAC, Lee changed its name upon assuming command on June 1, 1862, shortly after JOSEPH E. JOHNSTON was wounded at the Battle of Seven Pines; he would remain its commander throughout the rest of the war. Numbering approximately 120,000 when Lee assumed its leadership, the Army of Northern Virginia fought valiantly against overwhelming odds and, for the first few years of the war, won spectacular battles at SECOND BULL RUN, FREDERICKSBURG, and CHANCELLORSVILLE.

Lee's second failed northern invasion, which culminated in the Battle of GETTYSBURG at the beginning of July 1863, marked the turning point for the army and the Confederacy. The WILDERNESS campaign of the following spring decimated the Confederate troops; in one month, the army lost more than 30,000 on the battlefield, while disease and desertion took thousands more. By the time Lee surrendered at APPOMATTOX COURT HOUSE on April 9, 1865, the once-mighty Army of Northern Virginia numbered just 28,000 hungry, poorly clad soldiers, exhausted after three years of brutal war. (See ROBERT E. LEE and specific battles)

Confederate outer works. The structures in the left background, chevaux-de-frise, are made of sharpened stakes and used as infantry obstacles.

Orphan Brigade

Declared one of the best brigades in the army by top Confederate command, this Confederate unit of 4,000 hard-fighting Kentucky men earned its odd nickname because it originated in Kentucky, which remained a Union state throughout the war. The 1st Kentucky Brigade trained and organized in Tennessee, then defended their home state against Union general ULYSSES S. GRANT's offensive during the winter of 1862. In fact, the 1st Kentucky Brigade fought on its native soil for the last time in February, when Grant succeeded in pushing the Confederate army out of Kentucky. After being absorbed into the Army of Tennessee, the brigade fought at several major Civil War battles, including SHILOH, Corinth, VICKSBURG, CHICKAMAUGA, and throughout the ATLANTA CAMPAIGN. By the time the brigade surrendered at Washington, Georgia, in May 1865, its original members numbered just 500.

Pacifists

Thousands of citizens in both the North and South, mostly members of pacifist churches, objected to the Civil War on moral and/or religious grounds. In the nineteenth century, a number of so-called "peace churches," most prominently the Society of Friends (QUAKERS), with over 200,000 members, but also sects like the Mennonites, Shakers, and Dunkers, were thriving in America. With resolute tenets advocating nonviolence, they denied the obligation of military service. These beliefs were shared as well by individual members of churches without a pacifist canon, along with secular organizations like the New England Non-Resistance Society and utopian communities scattered across the country.

Because Quakers and other pacifists were among the most committed ABOLITIONISTS, the Civil War created a moral dilemma for them, especially after Lincoln's 1862 EMANCIPATION PROCLAMATION made the eradication of Confederate SLAVERY a war policy. Abolitionist leader WILLIAM LLOYD GARRISON, for one, who before the war had opposed the use of military force to achieve emancipation, guardedly supported Lincoln and the Union case. There were even a few dozen peace church members of military age who, facing reproach from their sects, volunteered for the army on both sides.

Other Confederate and Union pacifists alike engaged in nonmilitary work, including service in hospitals and industry; Northerners were often especially eager to teach and work with free blacks. Still, there were large numbers of conscientious objectors who opposed any kind of participation—including payment of taxes—in the war effort, and encountered vocal,

even violent, hostility toward their beliefs. The New England writer HENRY DAVID THOREAU was jailed for nonpayment of his taxes during the war, and was harassed by his community.

When conscription of soldiers was introduced in both the North and South, pacifists faced further pressures. The Union's draft laws did exempt conscientious objectors from combat, but required alternative service or an exemption fee. Pacifist groups denounced those conditions, even when Secretary of War EDWIN STANTON promised that their payments would be earmarked for an education fund for emancipated slaves.

Conscientious objectors remained subject to arrest and seizure of their property in some Northern communities, but the federal government routinely worked to release those who could prove membership in a peace church. Harder pressed for soldiers, the Confederate government tended to be less sympathetic to pacifists. QUAKER lobbyists did get the Conscription laws amended to allow nonservice options for peace

A music cover depicting pacifist sentiments.

church members, although those provisions were largely ignored as the war situation grew more desperate.

On both sides, pacifists unable or unwilling to buy their exemption found themselves in uniform. Sometimes deserting, sometimes simply refusing to take up arms, they created problems in the ranks. Although none was executed, rebellious pacifist soldiers were given punishments ranging from bread-and-water diets and sleep deprivation to beatings and assaults by bayonets. Regimental officers tended to come down hardest on conscientious objectors, while their superiors had took a more balanced approach. Recognizing that pacifists did not make good soldiers, most commanding generals simply wanted to send them home.

Parker, Ely

1828–1895

The highest ranking Native American officer in the Union army, Parker was present at the surrender of ROBERT E. LEE as a member of ULYSSES S. GRANT's staff.

Lieutenant Colonel Ely Parker

engineering degree from Rennselaer Polytechnic Institute in Troy, New York.

When the Civil War began, Parker was denied a commission in both the Union army and the New York state militia. In 1863, the army, now desperate enough for capable personnel to overcome its prejudice, reconsidered, and Parker was appointed division engineer under Brigadier General John Smith.

While serving at VICKSBURG, he became reacquainted with Ulysses S. Grant, whom he knew before the war, and joined Grant's staff during the 1864 PETERSBURG campaign as his military secretary with the rank of lieutenant colonel. Parker, despite his position, was not spared insult in the army, often referred to contemptuously by his fellow officers as "the Indian."

At the April 9, 1865, meeting between Grant and Lee at APPOMATTOX COURT HOUSE, he was responsible for transcribing the terms of surrender. The Confederate commander, according to witnesses, seemed startled by Parker's presence, evidently mistaking the dark-skinned Native American as a black man. Once he learned that

Parker was a full-blooded Seneca, born on a tribal reservation in New York. Although he had studied law, Parker was refused admittance to his home state's bar because he was not officially an American citizen. He then earned an

Parker (third from left) was an important member of General Grant's staff.

Parker was a Seneca, Lee commented, "I am glad to see one real American here." Parker's reply, famous in Civil War lore, was, "We are all Americans."

Continuing to serve on Grant's staff after the war, Parker became his aide-de-camp in 1867. As president, in a bold but controversial move, Grant appointed him Commissioner of Indian Affairs in 1869, a position that no Native American had ever previously held. Parker's tenure was a troubled one, however, as his department was plagued by corruption. A congressional investigation cleared Parker himself of any wrongdoing, but he was nevertheless compelled to resign. Suffering a series of setbacks in his subsequent business career, Parker died destitute in 1895.

Smoldering railroad iron, the work of Confederate partisans.

Partisans

Confederate guerrilla activity, designed to terrorize and undermine Union troops and operations, occurred almost from the beginning of the war and increased as the months and years of bloodshed dragged on. Fighting on their home turf, these army irregulars knew every mountain pass and path in the area and could strike suddenly at unsuspecting Union troops. Sometimes they attacked in small bands of just five or ten, sometimes in groups of several hundred. Their targets ranged from wagon trains and supply depots to Union outposts and camps.

In April 1862, the Confederate Congress, perhaps realizing that the Confederates could not win the war with the Regular army alone, enacted the Partisan Ranger Law. Calling for the formal organization of companies, battalions, and regiments of partisans, the Ranger Law entitled partisans to receive the same rations and allowances as regular soldiers. In addition, guerrillas would be paid the full value of any arms or ammunition they managed to capture from the enemy.

Partisan forces fought in both the Eastern and Western theaters. In the East, such clever and generally honorable men such as JOHN MOSBY, J. H. MacNeil, and Harry Gilmore fought a war of attrition against ULYSSES S. GRANT and PHILIP SHERIDAN. In the West the partisan fight, as led by WILLIAM CLARKE QUANTRILL, Bill Anderson, and George Todd, was distinctly more vicious. Quantrill, a former gambler and horsethief, and his men rampaged along the border of Kentucky and Missouri, robbing Union mails, ambushing Federal patrols, attacking boats on the Missouri River, and frequently murdering civilians they deemed disloyal to the Confederate cause. On August 25, 1863, Quantrill and about 300 others swept down upon the town of Lawrence,

Kansas, and slaughtered 17 Federal recruits and at least 150 Union civilians.

Apart from such blatant brutality, guerrilla warfare against the Union army was quite effective. In February 1863, ABRAHAM LINCOLN wrote, "In no other way does the enemy give us so much trouble, at so little expense to himself, as by the raids of rapidly moving small bodies of troops (largely, if not wholly, mounted), harassing and discouraging local residents, supplying themselves with provisions . . . and breaking our communications." The Confederate Congress repealed the Partisan Ranger Law in 1864, partly because of Quantrill's scourge at Lawrence and partly because partisans engendered jealousy among troops in the Regular army.

Partisans enjoyed relative freedom from military restrictions; living away from camp, they avoided most of the tedium experienced by Regular soldiers. In addition, their exploits—tricky maneuvers only possible if performed by a small group of men—soon became legendary. Despite the law's repeal, the Confederate secretary of war was authorized to allow certain bands to continue at his discretion, including Mosby and others in the Eastern theater. (See MOSBY'S RANGERS)

Patterson, Robert

1792–1881

General Robert Patterson was born in County Tyrone, Ireland, son of a veteran of the Irish Rebellion of 1798. The family came to America as a result of the elder Patterson's sentence of banishment following the uprising, and they settled in Pennsylvania. A volunteer in the War of 1812, Patterson distinguished himself on numerous occasions, rising through the ranks from an officer in the Pennsylvania militia to a captain in the Regular U.S. Army, serving with the 32nd Infantry Regiment. In civilian life, he was involved in business and government; he traveled extensively and kept a lively diary. When the MEXICAN WAR began, Patterson received a commission as major general of volunteers and distinguished himself at Cerro Gordo and Jalapa.

A railroad man and militia commandant during the intervening years, Patterson offered his services to his country at the outbreak of the Civil War. He was once again commissioned a major general of volunteers and was given command of the Department of Pennsylvania; later, he was given command of the Department of the Shenandoah, as well. Shortly before the BULL RUN campaign, Patterson was all that stood between JOSEPH E. JOHNSTON and the rest of the Southern troops in Virginia.

As Confederate forces began to concentrate beyond Washington, D.C., in the Manassas area in July 1861, Patterson was ordered to prevent Johnston from removing his troops from the valley. At the same time, President JEFFERSON DAVIS in RICHMOND, well aware of the threat Patterson represented on the valley front, nevertheless wired orders to Johnston to move his army to Manassas "if practicable." To Johnston's amazement, Patterson was discovered to have withdrawn on July 17 to Charles Town, in what is now West Virginia, rather than move toward Winchester in any effort to contain Johnston at all.

Other than a brief clash with Confederate cavalry on July 15,

Patterson made almost no movement to fulfill his mission and subsequently did not bring his own troops to the aid of General IRWIN MCDOWELL at FIRST BULL RUN on July 21, 1861. Nicknamed "Granny" by his disgruntled and embarrassed soldiers, Patterson received a far more stinging rebuke from Washington: he was relieved of command and replaced by Major General NATHANIEL S. P. BANKS. When questioned as to why he did not move as ordered, and why he did not assist McDowell, Patterson's response was that he had not received orders to attack.

Patterson's three-month commission was allowed to expire on July 27, 1861; the general returned to Philadelphia and pursued business matters for the rest of his life. He wrote an interesting account of his brief service, entitled *A Narrative of the Campaign in the Valley of the Shenandoah in 1861*. One of Patterson's six surviving children, Brigadier General Francis Engle Patterson, was accidentally killed by the unexpected firing of his own pistol on November 22, 1862, at Fairfax Courthouse, Virginia. The elder General Patterson is buried in Laurel Hill Cemetery, Philadelphia.

Peace Democrats

The Peace Democrats were a vocal group within the Democratic party who were opposed to saving the Union through military force. One of their supporters was CLEMENT VALLANDIGHAM, one of the so-called COPPERHEADS. The Peace Democrats wanted the swiftest possible end to the Civil War by means of peace conferences between the two opposing governments.

In the months leading up to the 1864 election, the Peace Democrats were successful in getting their party to agree to a "peace plank," or peace proposal, into the platform on which the party candidates would run for election; this plank stated that "immediate efforts be made for a cessation of hostilities," and detailed some of the means by which they would seek this result if elected.

The Democratic candidate for the presidency was General GEORGE B. MCCLELLAN; when he accepted the nomination of his party on September 8, 1864, he insisted that "the Union is the one condition of peace." He refused to agree to the peace plank unless it stipulated that any peace proposal should include the country being reunited. The Peace Democrats were split over this issue, some strongly believing that the war should end regardless of the cost, while others were just as insistent that the Confederacy not be recognized as an independent nation by any means but be made to rejoin the Union.

Ultimately, their platform would fail, very likely because of the split in policy; ABRAHAM LINCOLN would be reelected in November 1864, and the war would continue toward a military resolution that was still another six months away. (See WAR DEMOCRATS)

Peachtree Creek, Battle of

JULY 20, 1864

Peachtree Creek was one of the last-ditch efforts to preserve the city of ATLANTA, Georgia. As Union forces belonging to WILLIAM T. SHERMAN's army of the Cumberland converged on the capital from the north, and General John Schofield's Army of the Ohio moved in from the east along with JAMES MCPHERSON's

Army of the Tennessee, the Confederate defenders of the city under JOHN BELL HOOD made a stand against Sherman and his immediate subordinate, GEORGE H. THOMAS, hoping to successfully push them back before they could be reunited with the other two Union armies coming their way.

Thomas crossed Peachtree Creek the morning of July 20, 1864, and Hood ordered an attack—which inexplicably was delayed for three hours. Hood attempted to place the blame for the delay on General WILLIAM HARDEE. When the attack came, it was prolonged and bloody; but for all its valor the Confederate defense was ultimately a failure. After two hours, with nearly 20,000 men engaged on each side, the Southern losses were two and a half times greater than the North's. In the end, the Federals had Atlanta mostly surrounded; the only escape routes were to the south-southwest. The siege of Atlanta began two days later, after a bloody and costly battle around the city itself.

Pemberton, John Clifford

1814–1881

The man who was forced to surrender the Confederate stronghold of VICKSBURG on July 4, 1863, was a Northerner by birth. Despite his heritage, however, Pemberton fought hard and well for the Confederate cause; his failure at Vicksburg was due more to the conflicting orders he received from his commanders, President JEFFERSON DAVIS and JOSEPH E. JOHNSTON, than poor generalship on his part.

Pemberton was born into a family populated largely by antislavery, antiwar activists, including his father, who was a QUAKER minister. Somehow drawn to the military in spite of his family's PACIFISM, his application to West Point was successful in large part because of a long-standing friendship between his father and President Andrew Jackson.

Pemberton graduated in 1833, twenty-seventh in his class of 50. Appointed second lieutenant and assigned to the 4th Artillery, he first served in the Seminole War in Florida from 1837 to 1839, then performed garrison duty until the opening of the MEXICAN WAR. Twice brevetted for gallantry at Monterey and Molino del Rey, Pemberton had advanced to the rank of major by the end of the war. His longheld pro-Southern and pro-STATES' RIGHTS opinions were further solidified upon his 1848 marriage to Martha Thompson, the daughter of a wealthy Virginia family.

On April 24, 1861, he resigned from the army to accept Jefferson Davis' offer of a brigadier general's commission. His first assignment was as commander of the relatively minor Department of South Carolina, Georgia, and Florida. Earning two promotions, one to major general and the second to lieutenant general, he remained in the post until October 14, when he was given command of the Department of Mississippi and Louisiana.

Considering his reportedly less than inspiring personality and lack of command experience, some military historians see this appointment as one of "Jefferson Davis' major mistakes." With approximately 40,000 men, Pemberton faced the armies of ULYSSES S. GRANT and WILLIAM TECUMSEH SHERMAN, who were determined to capture the city of

General John C. Pemberton discussing the terms of surrender with Grant at Vicksburg.

VICKSBURG, thereby opening the Mississippi River to the North and cutting the Confederacy in half. In the winter of 1862, Pemberton's first advance stopped Grant at the Battle of Chickasaw Bluffs, during which the Federal army lost some 1,700 men.

Grant embarked upon a new approach in the spring, and Pemberton received contradicting sets of orders from his commanding officers in response to the renewed offensive. Joseph E. Johnston wanted Pemberton to abandon the city and save his army, while Jefferson Davis ordered Pemberton to hold the city at all costs. On May 14, Johnston sent word to Pemberton to come northeast and join him at Jackson, where he hoped they could defeat Grant together. Instead, Pemberton tried to stay close to Vicksburg and fight Grant from there. Just east of the city, Grant brought him to battle at Champion's Hill on May 16, beat him badly, and forced him back into Vicksburg with about 30,000 Confederates.

On May 22, the two-and-half month long siege of Vicksburg began. Pemberton watched his men grow ever more hungry and exhausted as Grant tightened his line around the city, cutting off communication and supplies. Finally, on July 3, Pemberton reluctantly gave the city over to the Federals, claiming that it would be "an act of cruel inhumanity to subject [the troops] any longer to the terrible ordeal."

Hoping to win easier terms of surrender, Pemberton shocked many Southerners by agreeing to allow the Union to declare victory on the national holiday of July 4. Some accused Pemberton of treason, pointing to his Northern roots as further proof of his disloyalty, but no formal charges were ever brought. Pemberton's men were indeed allowed to resign from the army and return home rather than face Federal imprisonment.

Following the surrender of Vicksburg, no command could be given Pemberton commensurate with his rank; he therefore resigned and accepted appointment as a colonel of artillery. At the end of the war, he settled for a time at Warrenton, Virginia, but finally returned to his home state of Pennsylvania, where he died on July 13, 1881.

Peninsula Campaign

MARCH–AUGUST 1862

The direct approach to the Confederate capital having failed at FIRST BULL RUN, commander-in-chief of the Federal armies, GEORGE B. MCCLELLAN, planned to attack RICHMOND, Virginia, by-passing what he believed was an enormous Confederate force led

General Fitz-John Porter's staff at the Virginia peninsula, including George A. Custer (lower right).

by Major General JOSEPH E. JOHNSTON at Manassas Junction. Transporting his men by ship down the Chesapeake Bay to the mouth of the Rappahannock, he would then lead them on foot across the peninsula to Richmond before Johnston could stop him. Although taking this course would leave Washington, D.C., exposed to the Rebel army, Lincoln—desperate for any action—agreed to the plan.

On March 17, McClellan began his advance. About 400 vessels carried more than 100,000 men from the Washington area to Fortress Monroe at the tip of the Virginia peninsula. Once ashore, however, poor weather, impassable roads, and flooding considerably slowed his march. On April 5, the Union advance reached Yorktown, where about 11,000 Confederates, led by the wily John Bankhead Magruder, waited in a solid defensive position.

Although vastly outnumbered by McClellan, Magruder used tricks—including marching one battalion in and out of a clearing several times—to convince McClellan that his force was enormous. Instead of attacking and annihilating his enemy, McClellan cabled Washington to send reinforcements. "It seems clear that I shall have the whole force of the enemy on my hands," he wrote, and informed Lincoln that he was settling in for a siege on Yorktown.

Lincoln begged the commander to push ahead, but McClellan refused. For more than a month, he did little more than wait, allowing Johnston to bring most of his army onto the peninsula to oppose his advance.

Nevertheless, McClellan's troops could still easily overwhelm Johnston's 60,000 men.

On May 3, with 100 Federal guns in place, McClellan was at last prepared to attack. That night, the Confederates surprised the Union army by launching a massive ARTILLERY attack. The surprise turned to shock in the morning when they realized that the Confederates had abandoned Yorktown during the barrage, retreating to a better defensive position to the south at Williamsburg. McClellan ordered his men to pursue and attack the Confederate line.

A brutal day of fighting ensued, with the Confederates losing about 1,700 men and the Union about 2,200, until the Rebels were forced to resume their withdrawal up the peninsula. By doing so, the Confederates essentially surrendered most of eastern Virginia, including Norfolk Naval Yard. The Confederate navy was forced to destroy its IRONCLAD, the CSS *Virginia (Merrimack)*, housed at the yard, to keep the Union from obtaining it.

By the end of May, the two armies opposed each other just outside of Richmond. McClellan again requested reinforcements;

A Multicultural Encyclopedia ☆ 481

Federal encampment at Cumberland Landing, Virginia, during the Peninsula Campaign.

specifically he wanted IRVIN MCDOWELL and his 40,000-man army to join him. McDowell, however, was occupied with the maneuvering of STONEWALL JACKSON in the Shenandoah Valley. On May 31, nature struck a blow against McClellan by flooding the Chickahominy River, thus isolating two Union corps near the villages of Fair Oaks and Seven Pines. Johnston immediately took advantage of the situation, ordering corps commanders James Longstreet and William Whitings to make a strong attack. In what one historian called "A Battle of Strange Errors," a series of miscommunications and mistakes on the part of the Confederates turned what might have been a victory into a draw. The day-long battle was a bitter one, however, killing or wounding more than 11,000 men—about 5,000 Federals and 6,000 Confederates.

The battle had two significant results. First, the fierce fighting frightened an already overcautious McClellan, who wrote home that he was "tired of the sickening sight of the battlefield with its mangled corpses and poor wounded." Second, the Confederate failure to fully exploit the situation caused President JEFFERSON DAVIS to replace Johnston with a more aggressive leader, ROBERT E. LEE.

Although McClellan continued to advance slowly during the next few weeks, his Peninsula campaign effectively ended when Lee assumed command. Lee did not plan to simply defend the Confederate capital, but instead devised his own offensive strategy known as the SEVEN DAYS CAMPAIGN, which pushed McClellan all the way back to HARRISON'S LANDING at the edge of the Potomac.

Perryville, Battle of

OCTOBER 8, 1862

This battle, Kentucky's only major conflict in the war, ranks as one of the stranger fights engaged in by Civil War soldiers. Fought essentially by accident, the battle was precipitated by a Confederate chance encounter with Union reconnaissance troops in search of water on a hot, terribly dry day. The commander of the Union forces at Perryville, the dapper General DON CARLOS BUELL, had been thrown from his horse the morning of the battle, and so had remained at headquarters taking a leisurely luncheon with General Gilbert, one of his subordinates. Owing to an atmospheric phenomenon concerning the terrain and the direction of the wind, the noise of the battle did not carry back in the direction of headquarters—with the result that Buell was unaware anything was going on and consequently did not field the majority of his troops until after four o'clock in the afternoon. His opponent, Confederate General BRAXTON BRAGG, did not fare significantly better; portions of his army were not present on the field either, still being in the vicinity of nearby Frankfort.

Bragg's second-in-command, Episcopal Bishop and Confederate General LEONIDAS K. POLK, very nearly got himself captured by the troops of the 87th Indiana Infantry (the Hoosiers), in yet another confused accident in the action of the day. Polk mistook the Hoosiers for Confederates and rode up to them with the command that they cease firing into the ranks of their own army. The 87th's commander, Colonel Shryock, responded with a demand to know who Polk was, since Shryock was certain his fire was directed appropriately. Polk realized he was speaking with the enemy, and made a hasty retreat before his confusion could lead to further embarrassment.

Buell's Federals managed to win the engagement despite the confusion. It was a costly defeat for the Confederates in terms of fighting force, as well as loss of territory; estimates of Bragg's casualties are near a fourth of his available 16,000 men. Buell's losses, on the other hand, taking into account that not all of his men even saw action, run just under one-tenth, with a little over 4,000 soldiers killed, missing, or wounded out of 37,000.

In the aftermath of Perryville, both Buell and Bragg would receive censure from their respective presidents, Buell for having failed to destroy the retreating Southerners, and Bragg for failing to hold Kentucky.

Buell was relieved of command; Bragg would keep his job a little while longer, owing almost entirely to the patronage of President JEFFERSON DAVIS. (See ACOUSTIC SHADOW)

Petersburg, Siege of

JUNE 1864–MAY 1865

The climax of the fighting in Virginia was an agonizing 10-month deadlock between deeply entrenched Union and Confederate forces, broken only when the worn-down Southern army was finally unable to withstand a frontal assault.

Nine days after his devastating defeat at COLD HARBOR in early June 1864, ULYSSES S. GRANT furtively began advancing the ARMY OF THE POTOMAC, leaving ROBERT E. LEE baffled about where the Federals were heading. Grant's target was Petersburg, the vital rail and communications center 20 miles south of RICHMOND through which most of the Confederate capital's supply lines ran. By capturing Petersburg, the Union commander recognized, he would ensure the capitulation of Richmond.

The 1st Pennsylvania Light Artillery on the front lines at Petersburg.

Army engineers, in an extraordinary feat of construction, briskly built a 2,100-foot pontoon bridge for the huge Federal force to cross the James River, and by June 15, William F. Smith's advance guard of over 10,000 was poised to begin the attack on Petersburg. Unaware that Confederate PIERRE G. T. BEAUREGARD had fewer than 2,500 men defending the heavily fortified city, the Union general struck far too cautiously, to the disgust of his troops. Smith still managed to make headway, coming close, in fact, to taking the town, but the Confederates held off the Federals until Lee and the ARMY OF NORTHERN VIRGINIA arrived to fill Petersburg's expansive trenches.

His chances for a quick victory spoiled, Grant commenced a daily ARTILLERY bombardment of Petersburg and reluctantly settled in for what he knew would be a long siege. Lee was no happier about the situation. With his vastly outnumbered force pinned down in an urgent defense of the South's capital, the Confederate commander lost the mobility that had been his greatest advantage and suspected that it would be "a mere question of time."

Grant himself wasted little time in putting his superior numbers to use. Constructing a formidable labyrinth of trenches, the Federals extended their line in both directions, swinging down from due east of Richmond more than 40 miles around to the southwest of Petersburg. Lee was forced to do the same, dangerously attenuating Confederate defenses. The South was so desperate for able bodies to line its defenses that it resorted to using old men, boys—and two unwilling members of the Confederate cabinet.

Life in the trenches was brutal for both sides. Numbing boredom was accompanied by the constant threat from sharpshooters and artillery fire. Burrowed in dirt and filth, exposed to the summer heat and the winter cold, the troops suffered even greater losses through disease. But while the Federals were regularly reinforced and kept decently fed and supplied, the Confederates nearly starved, and with

thousands deserting or surrendering simply to get food, their numbers diminished further.

Yet, Lee's position was still sufficiently fortified to hold off a Union assault. One audacious attempt to break the Confederate defense in late July, the "Battle of the CRATER," was a fiasco. After a regiment of Pennsylvania coal miners set off a huge explosion in a 500-foot tunnel dug right under the enemy, advancing Union troops were pulverized when they were trapped in the deep hole created by the blast.

The Federals were more successful in tightening the stranglehold on the Southerners. In August, they captured one of Virginia's key lifelines, the Weldon Railroad, after a failed attempt two months earlier. In October, Union forces repulsed a Confederate attempt to retake two vital roads, though later in the month they were unable to seize the Southside Railroad. By late winter 1865, Grant's army had grown to nearly 125,000 with reinforcements, while Lee's had dwindled to under 50,000.

With the besieging Union forces threatening to encircle him, the Confederate

A captured Confederate encampment at Petersburg.

commander's one remote chance to survive involved leaving the Petersburg trenches and combining forces with JOSEPH E. JOHNSTON's army in North Carolina. On March 25, John B. Gordon launched an abrupt attack on the Union line east of the town in an attempt to force the Federals to pull back and to create a breach through which Lee's army could escape south. Capturing Fort Stedman and a half mile of Union trenches, the Confederates seemed close to a breakthrough, only to be forced back after rallying Union troops counterattacked.

To forestall any further such attempts, Grant sent a force miles to the west of the Confederate defenses, trying to stretch Lee's weakened line to the breaking point. On April 1, infantry and cavalry from both sides battled at the FIVE FORKS junction, and GEORGE PICKETT's Confederate division was routed. When Grant received word of the victory, he ordered the conclusive blow. At 4:30 A.M. the next morning, the Federals launched an overwhelming onslaught along the entire Petersburg front. The Confederates simply could not hold; Union troops smashed through their line at several points.

After sending word to JEFFERSON DAVIS that the Confederate capital had to be evacuated, Lee ordered his men to retreat. Petersburg was occupied the evening of April 2, Richmond the following day.

Meanwhile, Lee's army headed west along the Appomattox River—desperately searching for food and for a way to cut south to join Johnston—with Ulysses Grant and the Federals in close pursuit.

Pickets

Pickets in the Civil War were at the same time a very necessary segment of the armies and a nearly invisible object of annoyance and derision to their comrades.

They were the soldiers detailed to stand guard outside the perimeter of an encamped army, as a first line of defense against attack. Seldom if ever stationed at a watchpost alone, there were often as many as four or five soldiers per position; they were charged with keeping one another awake, alert, and ready to raise the alarm if the enemy came too close.

Night and day, these men would be posted as much as a quarter mile from camp or along the army's line of march; if the enemy were sighted, one or two of the pickets would remain quietly to watch them and take note of regimental or corps badges or information written on flags, while the other pickets

Pickets warming themselves over a fire.

would hurry into camp to report the enemy's presence to the commanding officer.

This was very often a thankless job, for those who were good at it tended to get stuck with the duty on a regular basis; comrades believed they had the easy life out on the picket line, smoking, talking, perhaps playing cards and taking the occasional forbidden drink of whiskey. But in actual fact, pickets were in constant danger of being killed or captured, for guard duty was a critical but deadly job.

If a soldier fell asleep at his post, he endangered his entire camp as well as himself. Pickets were a favorite target of snipers from both sides, because they knew it was possible to excite a general alarm by gunning one down and making the enemy think there was an attack coming. While they were responding to an imagined threat, a real one could erupt from an entirely different part of the line.

Perhaps the most common phrases associated with the duties of a picket are these: "setting pickets," which simply means placing groups of them on the edges of one's camp; "being picketed" to a certain place, which meant being assigned to a post; and "having one's pickets driven in," which refers to an encounter of a large body of the enemy and one's own picket post, requiring the pickets to run into camp to raise the alarm. A truly careful attacker could see to it the driving in of pickets was the first hint the enemy had of an impending assault, for by then it would almost be too late to prepare for a strong attack.

When an army was in camp, pickets were usually drawn from the ranks of the infantry, though the cavalry picketed their own camps in the main; on the march, with a whole army in motion, it was the cavalry's duty to "ride picket" along the roads and forests near the route to protect the army from attack. Once the cavalry raised an alert, they either fought it off on their own, to their great credit, or gave warning to the infantry commanders—who would then wheel their soldiers from lines of march into lines of battle, a truly daunting sight to an enemy who thought he had taken them by surprise. Many a great battle began in just that way, by virtue of armies and pickets stumbling into one another without warning.

Pickett, George

1825–1875

He neither ordered nor planned the assault, his troops comprised less than half of the attacking force, and the rest of his Civil War service was rather undistinguished, but because he spearheaded the gallant, doomed Confederate charge that climaxed

Major General George E. Pickett

the Battle of GETTYSBURG, George Pickett's enduring fame is assured.

Graduating at the very bottom of his West Point class, the elegant, almost foppish Virginian performed ably in the MEXICAN WAR and on the western frontier. After joining the Confederate army, he led the "Gamecock Brigade" in the PENINSULA CAMPAIGN, where he was seriously wounded during the SEVEN DAYS battles in June 1862. Though he was promoted to major general that October and was present at FREDERICKSBURG, Pickett saw little further action until Gettysburg.

Guarding the South's rear during much of the battle, he and his all-Virginian division did not arrive on the field until early the third day, July 3, 1863. JAMES LONGSTREET, ordered by Confederate commander ROBERT E. LEE to mount an all-out assault on the center of the Union line, asked Pickett, one of his favorite officers, to coordinate the attack.

Eager to lead the South to glory, he confidently launched the charge with Longstreet's dubious nodded assent at about 3 P.M. Pickett stayed to the rear, as was customary for a division commander, while his three brigades and another six under A.P. HILL—a force totaling over 14,000—marched deliberately over three-quarters of a mile of open field toward the waiting Federals.

In less than an hour, PICKETT'S CHARGE was over, a magnificent effort but the disastrous failure that Longstreet predicted, with barely half of the attacking troops making it back to the Confederate line. When Lee told him to ready his division for a Union offensive, Pickett had to inform the general, "I have no division."

He continued to serve under Lee in the PETERSBURG campaign. On April 1, 1865, Pickett's troops were nearly wiped out at the Battle of FIVE FORKS, presaging the fall of RICHMOND. After he was defeated again four days later at Sayler's Creek, Lee relieved him of his command just prior to the APPOMATTOX surrender.

Once wanted by the Union as a war criminal for executing deserters, Pickett eschewed further military service—turning down a marshalcy from President Grant and a generalship from the Khedive of Egypt—to work in insurance back in Virginia. He never forgot the sad outcome of Pickett's Charge and, overlooking his own enthusiasm for the gamble, blamed Robert E. Lee. "That old man," Pickett insisted stubbornly and simply, "had my division massacred."

Pickett's Charge

JULY 3, 1863

"Whatever my fate, I shall do my duty like a brave man," declared GEORGE PICKETT just before he led 14,000 Virginians across an open field in one last-gasp effort to win a Confederate victory at GETTYSBURG.

After troops led by Richard Ewell had been driven back from Culp's Hill and JEB STUART's attack on the Federal rear was foiled, the Confederates' last hope for victory centered on breaking through the Union center at Cemetery Ridge. All afternoon, the Confederates had bombarded the ridge with ARTILLERY fire. When an eerie silence descended on the field at about 3:00 P.M., Generals ROBERT E. LEE and JAMES LONGSTREET mistakenly assumed they had destroyed the Union batteries and ordered 14,000 Confederate infantry to move forward.

They emerged from the woods on Seminary Ridge and organized themselves into one mile-long

Pickett's charge on the Union center, July 3, 1863.

line, complete with mounted infantry and colorful battle flags. The only avenue of approach open to the Confederates was across a mile-wide, empty field. With parade-ground precision, the Confederates marched down a small hill. The Union battery had not been destroyed, however; they had merely been saving ammunition to thwart just such an assault.

Within moments after the Confederates started across the field, Union artillery fire began to mow down row after row of the Confederate column. When the thinned-out ranks were within a short distance of the Federal line, their REBEL YELLS could be heard above the thundering of guns as they made their last dash to the front. Although the first line of Federals was driven back upon the earthworks near the artillery, Union fire and a sudden, furious hand-to-hand battle finally stopped the charge. In less than an hour, more than half of the brave men of Pickett's Charge had been killed and nothing had been gained. The Union claimed victory at Gettysburg and Lee was forced to retreat. (See GEORGE PICKETT)

Pillow, Gideon Johnson

1806–1878

Gideon Pillow, MEXICAN WAR veteran and former law partner of President James K. Polk, was known to be a conniving, secretive, and specious leader. A conservative on the question of SECESSION, Pillow nevertheless sought and received a commission in the provisional army of the state of Tennessee. He later became a brigadier general in Confederate service and was second in command of the Southern forces at FORT DONELSON.

When ULYSSES S. GRANT's forces were about to prevail over the defenders of the fort, Pillow suggested the exhausted Confederates attempt a massed charge to cut through Grant's lines, a move which surely would have resulted in slaughter. He was outvoted in favor of surrender. His commanding officer, General John B. Floyd, did not wish to be responsible for the surrender of Donelson, so he passed command to Pillow. Pillow did not wish the duty, either, and handed command off to General Simon Bolivar

Buckner, who eventually faced Grant and gave up Donelson in February 1862 under the Union general's famous UNCONDITIONAL SURRENDER terms. During the surrender, Floyd and Pillow escaped from the venue, a move which brought them great discredit. Pillow was temporarily suspended for these actions and never again held a command position of any responsibility in Confederate service.

He returned to the practice of law after the war, and at his death was buried in Helena, Arkansas.

Pinkerton, Allan

1819–1884

The noted detective proved to be no military intelligence expert when he served as the Union's head of SECRET SERVICE. The son of a Scottish policeman, Pinkerton emigrated to the United States in 1842, settling in Illinois and becoming a staunch ABOLITIONIST whose home was a station on the UNDERGROUND RAILROAD. He originally worked as a cooper, but entered law enforcement after stumbling upon a counterfeiting ring. Named Chicago's first police detective in 1850, Pinkerton resigned the same year to form a private agency under his own name, with a watchful-eye logo that became synonymous with the profession. The business flourished, and while conducting investigations for the Illinois Central Railroad, Pinkerton became acquainted with the company's lawyer, ABRAHAM LINCOLN.

En route to the inauguration in 1861, he informed the president-elect about an assassination plot being hatched in Baltimore, rumors some suspected that he invented himself. Pinkerton arranged Lincoln's secret passage to Washington, getting him to his destination safely but earning the incoming president much derision for supposedly sneaking ignominiously into the capital under disguise. Lincoln was grateful to Pinkerton nevertheless, and in April the master detective was asked to organize secret service operations for the Union.

Excelling at counterespionage, he and his agents uncovered a Confederate spy ring in the nation's capital operated by

Allan Pinkerton

prominent Washington socialite Rose O'Neal Greenhow. While assigned to GEORGE McCLELLAN's Department of the Ohio, Pinkerton personally embarked on clandestine missions into the deep South. He came back east when McClellan was named commander of the ARMY OF THE POTOMAC and, often going under the code name "Major E. J. Allen," joined him on his spring 1862 PENINSULA CAMPAIGN in Virginia.

Including fugitive slaves among his operatives, Pinkerton attempted to collect information on Confederate troop strength and movement, but this kind of intelligence-gathering was not his strength. His reports wildly overestimated the force mounted against the Northern army by two to three times its actual size, confirming McClellan's mistaken fears that he was outnumbered. The Union commander used these erroneous counts to demand reinforcements and to justify stalling his advance, squandering his advantage and dooming the campaign in the process.

Returning to Chicago after McClellan was relieved of command in the fall of 1862, Pinkerton limited his further Civil War service to investigations of fraud among Union military suppliers. He continued to build his agency and won further fame writing 18 self-serving books about his detective work.

Polk, Leonidas

1806–1864

Having abandoned an early army career for the clergy, the Episcopal bishop returned to military service during the Civil War and rose to high Confederate command, more through the support of his close friend, JEFFERSON DAVIS, than through his battlefield achievements.

Polk, a tall, gallant figure, came from a prominent North Carolina family and was a relative of President James K. Polk. Graduating from West Point near the top of his class, he left the army after six months to study for the Episcopal ministry. Polk was ordained as a deacon in 1830 and in 11 years was named bishop of Louisiana, where he owned a plantation and 400 slaves.

At the start of the war, Davis, a former West Point classmate, convinced the staunch secessionist that he would lend great prestige and legitimacy to the Southern cause by serving with the Confederate army. Bishop Polk was made a major general and assigned to supervise the fortification of the Mississippi Valley.

Determined to be more than a figurehead, Polk raced against Union officer ULYSSES S. GRANT to occupy the river stronghold of Columbus, Kentucky, in September 1861. In the process, however, he violated the border state's neutrality, causing its legislature to throw its support to the North. Placed under his West Point roommate ALBERT SIDNEY JOHNSTON, Polk repelled Grant's attack on the citadel two months later and led four assaults against the Union general's troops the following April in the Battle of SHILOH.

As second-in-command to BRAXTON BRAGG at PERRYVILLE, he was promoted to lieutenant general. Although Polk continued serving with Bragg, the two did not get along. After the New Year's 1863 Battle of MURFREESBORO, Polk suggested that his superior be replaced, and nine months later Bragg was ready to court-martial him for his supposedly sluggish performance at CHICKAMAUGA. Standing behind his friend, Davis reassigned Polk to Mississippi, where, indeed showing a tendency for slowness, he was

Lieutenant General Leonidas Polk

unable to stop the advance of WILLIAM T. SHERMAN's forces from VICKSBURG.

The bishop did not forsake his clerical work altogether during his Civil War service, taking time to baptize both JOHN BELL HOOD and JOSEPH E. JOHNSTON and to perform celebrated raider John Hunt Morgan's wedding ceremony during lulls in the fighting. Leading a corps under Johnston during the 1864 ATLANTA campaign, Polk was killed at Pine Mountain on June 14, by a stray round of enemy ARTILLERY fire while conferring with his commander. Jefferson Davis considered his death one of the South's worst setbacks. But while Polk was well-liked and respected, not many other Confederates agreed with Davis' assessment.

Pope, John

1822–1892

A skilled and courageous commander, John Pope held command of the Union's Army of the Virginia (later the ARMY OF THE POTOMAC) just long enough to suffer defeat at SECOND BULL

RUN before being replaced by his predecessor, GEORGE B. MCCLELLAN.

Described by contemporaries as dashing and a fine horseman, Pope was also known to be arrogant, abrasive, and incapable of inspiring loyalty among his officers or troops. After graduating seventeenth in his West Point class of 1842, the former Illinois farmboy entered the MEXICAN WAR as part of the Corps of Topographical Engineers; for his actions there he was brevetted captain for gallantry. From 1846 until the opening of the Civil War, he worked as an army engineer in the West.

On May 17, 1861, Pope was appointed brigadier general of volunteers in Missouri, then given command of the Army of the Mississippi the following February. He and his army played a major role in the campaign to open up the Mississippi River to Federal navigation, helping to capture New Madrid and Corinth at the beginning of March 1862. Just a few weeks later, President ABRAHAM LINCOLN called the victorious and apparently aggressive young general east to take over the new Army of the

Virginia, a well-equipped, well-trained army that George McClellan, a hesitant and ineffectual general, resisted sending into battle.

Pope's first action was to issue a high-handed, condescending statement that alienated officers and soldiers alike. Addressed to his troops, the statement suggested that McClellan, whom the troops adored and whose dismissal outraged the ranks, had taken a faulty approach to the war and that the soldiers themselves had not performed well. Pope also encouraged his men to seize food and supplies from Virginia farms and suggested that anyone suspected of aiding the Confederacy be hanged for treason without trial. Such opinions earned him the enmity of some of the more circumspect Northerners and certainly that of every Southerner, including General ROBERT E. LEE, who described Pope as a "miscreant."

That Pope entered the eastern theater at a time when the Confederates had the upper hand did not help matters, either. After pushing the Federals back

Brigadier General John Pope

from RICHMOND during the SEVEN DAYS CAMPAIGN in the spring, Lee made a daring move to invade the North. Lee's brilliant strategy simply overwhelmed the relatively inexperienced commander. When the armies met from August 28 to September 2, Lee's 55,000 troops outmaneuvered and outfought Pope's Army of the Virginia at SECOND BULL RUN. The next day, Lincoln removed Pope from command, replacing him with the problematic but beloved "Little Mac" McClellan.

Pope's Civil War career effectively ended; he was sent to command the Department of the Northwest, where he became somewhat of an expert in Indian affairs. Promoted major general in the U.S. Army in 1882, Pope retired four years later. He died at the Old Soldiers' and Sailors' Home in Sandusky, Ohio, September 23, 1892.

Porter, David Dixon

1813–1891

By the time the Civil War began, 48-year-old David Porter, soon to become one of the greatest naval heros of the war, had been engaged in naval affairs for more than 35 years.

A member of the most distinguished family in United States naval history, David Dixon Porter literally grew up on the sea. At the age of 10, he accompanied his father, a naval officer and diplomat, on an expedition to suppress piracy in the West Indies. At the age of 14, he was made midshipman in the Mexican Navy. In 1829, Porter returned to the United States and joined the navy, serving in the Mediterranean and the South Atlantic. First as lieutenant and then as commander of the *Spitfire*, Porter took part in every coastal engagement during the MEXICAN WAR from 1846 to 1848.

On April 1, 1861, he was given command of the powerful steamer the *Powhatan* and sent to the Gulf of Mexico, a promising start to his Civil War service. As commander of the *Powhatan*, Porter sailed to the Gulf of Mexico to relieve Fort Pickens at Pensacola, Florida, which had been under siege for several months. He stayed in the gulf for the remainder of the war's first year.

To assist DAVID FARRAGUT's assault on New Orleans in April

Admiral David Dixon Porter

1862, Porter led a flotilla of small sailing vessels, equipped with mortar and shells, into the harbor in hopes of diminishing Forts Jackson and St. Philip. His plan failed, however, and Farragut's larger, more powerful fleet was necessary to take the forts; the forts finally surrendered on April 28, 1862.

Two months later, Porter was appointed acting rear admiral of the Mississippi Squadron and assumed naval responsibility for the Mississippi and its northern tributaries. His first action, taken in cooperation with WILLIAM TECUMSEH SHERMAN, was to capture the Arkansas Post in January 1863, thereby opening the Mississippi to Federal navigation. In the spring, Porter assisted ULYSSES S. GRANT in his move against VICKSBURG. In one attempt to reach the city, Porter sailed his fleet from the Mississippi through Steele Bayou, then into and across the Yazoo River below the heavily fortified Fort Pemberton. Porter's gunboats, however, were caught in the narrow, swampy streams that crisscrossed the region. When Confederates began felling trees behind the fleet in an attempt to trap the Union ships, Porter was forced to call to Sherman for army support. Once extricated, Porter headed back to the Mississippi, his first mission at Vicksburg a failure.

On April 30, however, he came through for Grant by taking a dozen vessels loaded with supplies and soldiers across the Mississippi through heavy Confederate gunfire. The passage took more than two hours, but Porter managed to lose just one transport. For his actions at Vicksburg, he was promoted to rear admiral and given increased responsibility for a larger territory: the Mississippi River system north of New Orleans.

The spring of 1864 found Porter ready to undertake what was to be a dreadful failure for the Federal forces during the RED RIVER CAMPAIGN. Nature and poor planning scuttled the mission to secure the important river for the Federals. Porter nearly lost his fleet during the expedition, but managed to save most of his ships. In October 1864, Porter was sent east to take command of the North Atlantic Blockading Squadron, which was responsible for blockading the coast north of South Carolina. Under orders from Grant to capture Fort Fisher at Wilmington, Porter and army Brigadier General Alfred H. Terry planned a combined naval-land offensive.

On the morning of January 14, 1865, Porter's fleet of 40 warships—the largest ever assembled—began to bombard the fort. At 4:00 P.M., 1,600 of Porter's sailors and 400 marines stormed the northeastern end of the fort while brigades of infantry scaled the parapet. Fierce hand-to-hand combat continued for several hours, until the garrison

Sherman's conference with Grant, Lincoln, and Porter aboard the River Queen.

finally fell at 9:00 P.M., closing the Confederacy's last open port on the East Coast.

After his victory at Fort Fisher, Porter's Civil War career ended, but he continued to serve in the military for the rest of his life. He was promoted to vice-admiral in 1866 and to admiral in 1870. He served as superintendent of the Naval Academy for several years before being appointed head of the Navy Department. David Dixon Porter's remarkable life-long record as a naval officer appeared to run in the Porter family. David Farragut, under whom he served at the capture of NEW ORLEANS, was his foster brother. Another brother, Commodore William D. Porter, assisted ANDREW H. FOOTE as commander of the *Essex* in the campaign up the Tennessee River early in 1862. Porter's cousin, FITZ-JOHN PORTER, another promising Civil War officer, won accolades for his performance as a soldier during GEORGE MCCLELLAN'S PENINSULA CAMPAIGN, but gained many detractors after SECOND BULL RUN. Author of several books about his remarkable life, Porter remained active until his death at the age of 78. (See NAVY)

Porter, Fitz-John

1822–1901

The story of Union General Fitz-John Porter must surely rank as one of the most frustrating and difficult in the annals of the war. Born to a Portsmouth, New Hampshire, navy family that included Commodore David Porter and Admiral DAVID DIXON PORTER, young Fitz-John nevertheless chose the army, graduating from West Point high in his class in 1845. He served for a time in the 4th Artillery, until the outbreak of the MEXICAN WAR took him to that training ground for future Civil War generals. Serving under Zachary Taylor,

Porter was later transferred to WINFIELD SCOTT's army, with whom he saw action from Vera Cruz to Mexico City. He was brevetted for gallantry at Molino del Rey and Chapultepec, and finished the war with a rank of major.

From 1849 to 1855 he was an instructor at West Point, teaching ARTILLERY and cavalry tactics. Eventually returning to more active service, Porter was involved in the 1857 MORMON Expedition to Utah, where he served with many men who would later fight alongside or opposite him in the Civil War. On the eve of the nation's breakup, Porter was assigned to numerous difficult tasks associated with the secession of the Confederate states: inspecting Charleston's defenses, lest it should become necessary to level them; finding the means to withdraw loyal troops from Texas after that state's secession; and keeping the trains running between Washington City and the Northern states.

When the fighting began, Porter received a number of assignments, including an appointment on May 17 as brigadier general of Volunteers, and was sent to fight with

General Fitz-John Porter and staff, June 1862.

NATHANIEL BANKS and ROBERT PATTERSON in the Shenandoah Valley. During GEORGE MCCLELLAN'S PENINSULA CAMPAIGN, Porter, who was initially an intimate of McClellan, rose from division command under General Heintzelman to command of the 5th Corps. Attacked in force at Mechanicsville and GAINES MILL, Virginia, during the drive to take RICHMOND, Porter offered a valiant defense of his position; after a hard fight, he withdrew in good order across the Chickahominy River. Porter's corps was responsible for the safety of the wagon train as McClellan finally began moving across the peninsula, and had orders to occupy and hold Malvern Hill as a protective point for the entire Union army in the campaign.

McClellan's troops were later reassigned to Major General JOHN POPE, in the Union entity known as the Army of Virginia. Porter's men reached the rendezvous by way of the Rappahannock River at Falmouth, Virginia—just in time to receive the brunt of a startling attack by ROBERT E. LEE and STONEWALL JACKSON, as they moved Jackson's corps in an attempt to skirt Pope's right flank and break for Thorofare Gap. It took Pope some time to realize what was afoot, whereupon he sent Porter to try and contain the elusive Jackson before he could reunite with the rest of Lee's army. The plan was to attack Jackson's right flank on August 29, 1862, and defeat him before turning to deal with JAMES LONGSTREET, but Porter failed to follow through on this task. At SECOND BULL RUN (Second Battle of Manassas), Jackson was able to decisively defeat Pope on the old familiar battlefield, sending the scattered and demoralized Northerners back to WASHINGTON, D.C., where the army was reshuffled and Porter's corps was returned to McClellan's command.

The following November, General Porter was relieved of command and summoned to a court martial; the charges, leveled by John Pope, included failure to obey orders, disloyalty, and misconduct in the face of the enemy, any one of which was a serious charge all on its own. Pope was clearly looking for a scapegoat, and though Porter offered a rigid defense along the lines that Pope had not given clear orders at any time, and that the Confederates had been in such position as to render impossible the orders he did receive, he was found guilty and dishonorably dismissed from the army on January 21, 1863— coincidentally the thirty-ninth birthday of Stonewall Jackson, the author of Porter's troubles.

Porter began immediately trying to clear his name, but was unable to secure a review of the proceedings until 1879. The wait was worth it, for a board of generals appointed to look into the matter found in Porter's favor. However, it was not until 1882 that the president took some action on Porter's behalf; part of

Harper's Weekly *sketch of Porter's court martial, December 1862.*

the sentence was remitted to allow him to hold office in the United States. During this time, ULYSSES S. GRANT wrote an unsolicited testimony in Porter's favor, publishing an article in the *North American Review*, "An Undeserved Stigma." Four years later, on August 5, 1886, ironically owing to the intervention of Congressman JOSEPH WHEELER, formerly a Confederate cavalry commander in the Army of Tennessee, Porter was reappointed to the rank of colonel of infantry from May of

1861—unfortunately without remuneration of back pay—and then was promptly placed on the retired list two days later.

Porter was finally able to get on with his life and moved to Colorado, where he was involved in mining. He had not been entirely idle during the years that he spent waiting for exoneration, however; he ran a mercantile business in New York, and reluctantly turned down an offer from the Khedive of Egypt of command of the entire Egyptian Army. Porter held such disparate positions as construction superintendent for the State Asylum in New Jersey; receiver of accounts for the Central Railroad of New Jersey; and public works, fire and police commissioner for the city of New York. At the age of seventy-nine, General Porter died of natural causes in Morristown, New Jersey, leaving behind a widow and four children.

Potomac, U.S. Army and Department of the

The North's most famous army in the Civil War lost more men, proportionately, than any army before or since. Nevertheless, it emerged victorious after APPOMATTOX and its service to the United States reached legendary status almost immediately.

Charged with protecting Washington and capturing

Army of the Potomac before Chancellorsville.

RICHMOND, the Army and Department of the Potomac was created on August 15, 1861. Until that time, it had been known as the Military District, then the Military Department, of the Potomac. The number of corps attached to it, and the geographical area it covered, would fluctuate during four years of war, as would its commanders.

The first to take the helm of "Mr. Lincoln's Army" was GEORGE B. MCCLELLAN, who instilled a sense of displine, pride, and respect for training the army retained throughout the war. After McClellan failed to make headway during his PENINSULA CAMPAIGN or stop Lee's advance during the SEVEN DAYS CAMPAIGN, President ABRAHAM LINCOLN reorganized

Generals McClellan and Burnside with the Army of the Potomac at Rectortown, Virginia, November 10, 1862.

his command, splitting off the Army of the Potomac and creating a new Army of the Virginia headed by JOHN POPE.

After Pope lost at SECOND BULL RUN, Lincoln returned McClellan to command and the Army of the Potomac remained the largest army in the North ever after. When McClellan again failed to take aggressive action following his victory at ANTIETAM, AMBROSE EVERETT BURNSIDE took command and led the now battle-ready troops to their third major loss at FREDERICKSBURG. Immediately following the debacle, he was replaced with JOSEPH E. HOOKER, who led the army to another devastating defeat at the hands of ROBERT E. LEE at CHANCELLORSVILLE.

On June 28, 1863, Lincoln chose GEORGE GORDON MEADE, who had proven himself an able and consistent corps commander during the first two years of the war, to head the army. It won its first major victory at GETTYSBURG, in July 1863. Although Meade perhaps missed an opportunity to crush Lee's forces by not vigorously pursuing them after the defeat, the battle was nonetheless a turning point both in the war and in the fortunes of the Army of the Potomac itself.

After ULYSSES S. GRANT was appointed lieutenant general-in-chief of all the Union forces, the Army of the Potomac went on to victory at PETERSBURG, RICHMOND, and at APPOMATTOX, where Lee finally surrendered. On May 23, 1865, the Army of the Potomac was formally disbanded.

Prisoner Exchange

Captured soldiers of both the North and South languished in deplorable prison camps once the delicate prisoner exchange program fell apart over the Confederacy's refusal to include black troops in the deal and the Union's realization that the policy aided the enemy's war effort.

Field officers had informally traded captives after battles since the early days of the conflict. With a far smaller reserve of able-bodied men and with fewer resources to keep prisoners, the South was eager to formalize the arrangement. Although ABRAHAM LINCOLN hesitated entering into an agreement that would tacitly recognize the Confederacy, he was swayed by public pressure, and an official exchange cartel was concluded in July 1862. The policy called for captured soldiers of equal rank to be traded on a one-for-one basis, with four privates equaling one lieutenant, 60 a commanding general, and so forth.

Despite occasional disputes, most concerning when and whether released prisoners could return to armed service, the arrangement lasted for ten months, freeing about 200,000. The breakdown came when African-American troops began serving in the Union army. Outraged at what it saw as the arming of fugitive slaves, the Confederate Congress in May 1863 declared that captured black soldiers, fugitive or not, would be reenslaved and that they—and their white commanders—could also be subject to execution. The North, demanding that the captured blacks be acknowledged as legitimate prisoners of war and included in exchanges, promptly suspended the agreement and the Union and Confederate prison camp populations swelled.

Rations served to exchanged Union prisoners on board the New York.

Late that year, the South altered its stance by promising that only actual runaways would be returned to bondage, but the impasse remained. ULYSSES S. GRANT reiterated the North's position in an April 1864 order, stating that "no distinction whatever will be made in the exchange between white and colored prisoners." Some claimed that the Union's new general-in-chief had another purpose in mind—that he was willing to sacrifice thousands of soldiers to the enemy's prisons because the South would be hurt even more by the depletion of manpower.

Desperate inmates at ANDERSONVILLE prison sent petitions to Lincoln urging him to resume prisoner exchanges, physicians and clergymen lobbied the president as well, and the Democrats tried making the government's "cruel" inflexibility into an election issue. But Lincoln, believing the principle outweighed the suffering, would not yield. Finally in January 1865, as the faltering Confederacy was contemplating the use of armed slaves in its own military, it agreed to include blacks in prisoner exchanges. By the time the practice resumed, with three months left in the war, nearly 50,000 captured soldiers had died in prison. (See CONFISCATION ACT, PRISON LIFE)

Prison Life

One of the difficult realities of military service in the Civil War was the ever-present possibility that a soldier might be taken prisoner as a result of action undertaken by his regiment.

Because this war took place during the Victorian Era, a time of great civility, there was very little mistreatment of prisoners on the actual field of battle; the men of the two armies seemed to instinctively understand they could just as easily have been in the other fellow's shoes, and so behaved toward captured enemy soldiers with a polite gentlemanliness. If captured, one could expect to be required to give one's parole: that is, to make some sort of promise not to attempt to escape. If offered and accepted, parole made it possible for the captives to be sent back under flag of truce to their own lines—whereupon the paroled soldiers would be sent home until an exchange was effected between the Confederate and United States governments,

Overcrowded conditions at Andersonville Prison.

allowing the parolees to return to active duty. If a paroled soldier went back to the field unexchanged, he was liable to be shot, or in times of low ammunition, hanged, for having broken one of the more curious and seldom transgressed gentlemen's agreements of the army tradition.

As the war went on, however, the simple parole of captured soldiers became a less often seen phenomenon. It became the policy of the Union in 1864 to cease offering exchanges altogether, in hopes of wearing down Confederate resistance by draining their manpower. Confederate soldiers captured in battle were most often sent to prisons in the North. Some of the best-known Union prisons were Point Lookout, Maryland; Johnson's Island, the Ohio State Penitentiary, and Camp Chase, Ohio; and Rock

Island, Illinois; in the South, there was a Union prison mostly for captured Confederate officers at Fortress Monroe, Virginia. Confederate prisons included Danville, Virginia; Camp Oglethorpe, Georgia; Mobile, Alabama, and Salisbury, North Carolina. Prisons in the South were constructed wherever there was room; Libby prison in RICHMOND was a converted tobacco warehouse, while the infamous ANDERSONVILLE was in a field in Georgia.

Until fairly recently, it was widely believed that Confederate prisoners in Northern hands were treated decently, fed abundantly, and sent home in good physical condition, while Union prisoners in Southern facilities were starved, brutalized, beaten, and murdered. In each case, there is exaggeration.

Men of rank could generally expect a certain level of good treatment, as the officer in charge of the prison could be expected to sympathize with a fellow

Three Confederate soldiers after their capture at Gettysburg.

officer. Many an officer both North and South was indeed fed well, treated well, and—oddly enough—was frequently given a new uniform upon his exchange, minus the military buttons. And there are ample stories of acts of kindness and gentlemanly conduct between prisoners and their keepers; the otherwise loathed Union General BENJAMIN BUTLER went to great difficulty to find a warhorse belonging to ROBERT E LEE's son, cavalry brigadier WILLIAM H. F. LEE, which had been stolen from him during his capture in 1863. As there is almost always a reverse side to the coin, however, one must look at the brutal treatment accorded to the brother of Confederate raider John Hunt Morgan (see MORGAN'S RAIDERS), when he was captured during an expedition into the Ohio Valley. Incarcerated in the Ohio State Penitentiary, Morgan and his companions were stripped, had their heads shaved, and were imprisoned in cells that were 38 inches wide by six and a half feet long; when it was believed they might try to escape, they were put into unheated cells at one end of the prison with no blankets or beds, and no room to move in order to warm

themselves, in sub-zero weather. They languished in this state for 16 days, because they would not confess the details of an escape plan no one was entirely certain even existed.

The 35,000 men incarcerated in Andersonville could certainly speak of the horror of being a prisoner of war, and there was general acclaim at the war's conclusion when the commandant, HENRY WIRZ, became the only Confederate official actually prosecuted for war crimes. Undeniably terrible as the overcrowded conditions in Andersonville were, Wirz was not entirely lacking an explanation for his actions: the Confederate Congress passed a law stating that prisoners were to have as their daily ration the same allowances made for Southern soldiers in the field, and they were starving as well. As for medical supplies for the prisoners, there were none to be had—as a result of the Northern blockade of Southern ports. The unhappy fact of life for prisoners on both sides was that measures taken to shorten the war often trickled down to those who were least able to take action for their own comfort and safety. (See PRISONER EXCHANGE, RICHMOND)

About the Civil War Society

The Civil War Society, whose headquarters are located in Berryville, Virginia, is comprised of over 65,000 Civil War scholars, students, writers, collectors, and reenactors. The organization's mission is to further historical research and preserve historic sites and battlefields. Its bimonthly publication, *Civil War: The Magazine of the Civil War Society*, disseminates the cutting-edge research and analysis of Civil War Society contributors throughout the country. Through the Civil War Society's extensive fundraising efforts, the organization has been able to donate monuments to and restore major battlefields throughout the region torn apart by war over a century ago. Its educational outreach program organizes an extensive lecture and workshop series, and sponsors walking tours of historical sites.